Praise for *How to Save Money on Legal Fees: Separation and Divorce*

As a family lawyer I am always looking for ways to help my clients navigate what is often a painful, complex, daunting, confusing and expensive process. I feel that we have a professional and moral obligation to be the best we can be for the sake of our clients. This book will not only save clients money (because it helps them understand the process, ask questions and consider what is truly important to them) it will also demystify the process for them and empower them. This book is an essential read and tool for family lawyers who are passionate about their profession and care for their clients and one to be recommended to all Family Lawyers and their clients. Adrian, I applaud you for your valuable resource and considerate insight into what is a painful process for most family law clients. This is a book that has been desperately needed for a long time.

— Gail Allison, Principal, *Pathway Legal*

Congratulations to Dr Adrian Callum on this fabulous book. Adrian Callum has carefully and critically examined the intricacies of separation and divorce—the whys, the lies, the consequences. She has put together the most useful resources for anyone involved in relationship breakdown. This book offers advice, insights and practical checklists for individual and family law practitioners alike. This book is a useful tool if your separation is a high conflict or amicable one. It helps you identify what is really important in the process of separation, how to stay focused and achieve your desired outcomes. This book will certainly help any reader save money on their separation and divorce—and be the best version of themselves along the way.

— Jennifer Franklin, Principal, *Franklin Family Law*

Separation and divorce can be the darkest period of someone's life. Some don't survive it. Any helping hand is welcome and Dr Adrian Callum's book, *How to Save Money on Legal fees: Separation and Divorce* offers this, with both empathic and expert advice, looking after the person as well as helping to save money on daunting legal costs—a major source of stress. This book belongs in the hands of every helping professional.

— Dr Robyn Wilson, General Practitioner

This is a book that not only gives clients a voice. It gives them power.

— Garry Goodey, Community Development Consultant

This book is compelling. It delivers on its promise to help us save money on our separation. Read it and give copies to people you love.

— Linda H. (recently separated)

Books rarely cause a raging reaction in book clubs. This one did. The blinding consensus was 'I wish I had read this book before I divorced!'.

— Petra K., Marilyn R., Rosie T., Jane F., Sonya Z, and Susan G.

Adrian Callum clearly wants the best for separating couples.She is so totally focused on clients of family lawyers. This book is easy to read (no jargon), rich in empathy, reassurance and confidence-building. What a great guide - what to expect, how to prepare, what to do, and what to say. The book has lots of resources. It even deals with the tasks about which we have no clue - how to instruct a lawyer, how to bargain, and establishing boundaries for communication. Resources and contact details are spread throughout the book. They are also on her website. Stuff about which so many of us are clueless. There are so many lightbulb moments. I bought several copies of this book from her website, including two for my parents!

— Sean Kelly, Social Worker

HOW TO SAVE MONEY ON LEGAL FEES

SEPARATION & DIVORCE

ADRIAN CALLUM

How to Save Money on Legal Fees: Separation and Divorce
A **Law & Life** Book

First published in 2021 by Law & Life Pty Ltd. Second edition published 2022 by Law & Life Pty Ltd.
PO Box 90, Greenslopes QLD 4120
www.lawandlife.com.au

A catalogue record for this work is available from the National Library of Australia.

NATIONAL LIBRARY OF AUSTRALIA
A catalogue record for this book is available from the National Library of Australia

Cover Design: Luke Harris
Text Design and Typesetting: Luke Harris
Editor: Rebecca Wylie

ISBN: 9781925669008 (pbk)
ISBN: 9781925669015 (ebook)

The author and the publisher would like to thank the following copyright holders, organisations, individuals for their permission to reproduce copyright material in this book: © Jess Hill author of *See What You Made Me Do*; © Paul Clitheroe, author of *Money, Marriage and Divorce*; © Australian Institute of Family Studies; © Clarissa Rayward author of *Splitsville.*

Disclaimer

Contents

Preface

How this book will help you

Relationship separation hurts. This we all know. The pain of loving and losing can seem insurmountable. The last thing anyone wants at this time are big bills for services that come with such a challenging life change.

How to Save Money on Legal Fees: Separation and Divorce makes it easier for you to navigate the complex world of family law and still feel some sense of control. It can help you shape the future you want, and it can also help you save many thousands of dollars in legal fees. It is full of resources and tools you can use to make your separation process easier. All forms and tables you see in the book will be available for you to download from my website: **www.lawandlife.com.au**

This book does not pull its punches.

Mounting legal fees is a fear that many experience. Regardless of your background, legal fees blowing out and depriving you of the ability to care for yourself and others is terrifying. If you are a parent, you just want a better life and to give your kids more opportunities than you had growing up. Being sunk in poverty can have lasting effects. And if you are a parent, you may end up with lifelong guilt if you do not handle your separation with your future in mind. But here's the thing:

This fear can be managed. Saving money can be achieved so you can look after yourself and your kids.

Lawyers are sometimes a good punching bag. We know from media coverage, academic research, client experience, and reports by agencies which regulate lawyer conduct, that lawyers do not always do the right thing by their clients. Some misappropriate trust fund money, some act unethically, some overcharge clients, some inflate the numbers of hours worked on your matter, and so on. And while I am quick to point out the risks of dealing with unethical lawyers, a great family lawyer—and there are plenty of them—will get you through your separation in good financial shape. Consulting a lawyer is an undertaking which requires careful consideration. This book teaches you how to do this.

How to Save Money on Legal Fees: Separation and Divorce is designed for *you*, whether you are planning, currently experiencing, or recovering from relationship separation. I have provided checklists, insights, information and exercises to help you upskill your approach to your separation, encourage clear thinking and aid smart decision-making.

Where you live doesn't matter

Although the examples of the separation process used in this book often draw on the Australian context, *this book is for you wherever you live.* The content of this book can apply to Australia, New Zealand, United Kingdom, Canada and the United States, but anyone from anywhere can take value from the book's information, tools, resources, planning, skills development, communication tactics, and attitude. It's about saving *you* money through good decision-making.

That said, one section of this book deals with legal options for finalising your relationship. If you reside in the countries mentioned above, you will have similar options and broadly similar processes. I am therefore confident that you will derive great value from engaging with this book. If you are keen to learn more about your state/country's family law system you can consult your local Law Society.

I am not going to overwhelm you with legal complexities, rules and applications, and Court decisions in this book. I am dedicated to showing you how to *navigate* them. When the time comes for you to engage legal assistance, it will be your family lawyer who will explain legal rules relevant to your particular situation.

Impatient to learn more about how this book will help you? Let's get to the benefits of the book.

Benefits of this book

- You can save heaps of money to dedicate to your new future.
- You can save money to care for your kids without financial worry.
- You can save time, and time means money.
- You can quickly learn how to act with purpose and remain in control of your separation process.
- The practical management of your legal separation process is laid out for you.
- Your confidence will soar with the step-by-step guide to preparing for separation so that you can achieve the outcomes you want.
- Your ability to be across every aspect of your process will be guided by advice on what documents you need for your lawyer and how to arrange them.
- You can learn how to choose the right lawyer for you.
- You can learn how to interact with your lawyer, so you keep saving money and move forward.
- You can use the communication skills you learn to influence outcomes at all stages of your separation process.
- And more ...

Sections

This book is divided into seven sections.

The first section, *Separation,* offers you opportunities to understand the legal meaning of separation, and the facts, rather than the myths, which prevail about who 'wins'. The section also guides you through the four steps of the property division process and how it actually works for you and your Ex. Should you have the option of preparing to separate, you will be shown the tasks that can help you. The final chapter in this first section addresses how to make sound decisions that can shape favourable outcomes for your future.

The second section, *Disclosure,* guides you through the importance of documents in the legal process of your separation. It lists the documents you will need to give to your family lawyer. This section will also discuss deceit, and how it can present during your separation. You will be alerted to the signs of deceit and shown how to tell if your Ex is being deceitful in a way which can disadvantage you in your property division.

The third section, *Smart communication,* spotlights core communication skills during the separation process that you will need to draw on in order to save money. It comes before sections four and five, which focus on your legal pathways, because you will need your communication skills for those stages. It is often said that the separation process is a crash course in learning to communicate with your Ex in the cold light of day through the lens of finance. With sharpened communication skills you will derive great value from this section's chapters on how to persuade your Ex to choose the most productive legal pathway for your separation. You will also learn how to make the most of asking questions, listening, and using silence in your interactions with your Ex.

The fourth section, *Legal pathways,* addresses the typical legal pathways to separation available to you, the processes involved, and their advantages and disadvantages. I have also spotlighted two sensitive issues which often emerge in negotiations: parenting plans and pet custody. In the rawness of separation, each of these issues can derail your separation process if not handled with care. The final chapter in this section draws your attention to costs and consumer issues. All chapters in this section are designed to foster your ability to get going with confidence, and with enough information to achieve your goal of saving money.

The fifth section, *Choosing the right lawyer for you*, focuses on your interactions with your family lawyer. This section tackles confronting questions. How will you choose your family lawyer? How will you work with your family lawyer armed with the knowledge you have learned from this book? I have provided you with sample scripts to give you a sense of what to say and how to say it. This section explains how you can gain greater value from working with your family lawyer using your awareness of the dynamics between client and lawyer. If you have insight into your role as a client, you can better drive the separation process. All of this is designed to save you money on legal fees.

The sixth section of this book addresses the issue of *Help*. How do you find the help you need? How do you identify the many support services available to you? This section will show you how accessing help can protect your income, attend to the tasks that need doing, especially if you have kids to care for, keep going to work, and most of all, look after yourself so that you can stay in shape and maintain control of your life. The second chapter in this sixth section is for those who may need the help of a skilled psychologist to process this period of intense change. I appreciate that seeking the help of a psychologist can be intimidating for some, so I have provided step-by-step guidance to demystify the process of what it is like to consult a (good) clinical psychologist. Getting help is a sound investment. When you manage your stress, your decision-making improves and can lead to better financial decisions.

The final section of this book, *Conclusion*, spotlights what you can do with all of the money you have saved on legal fees. It shows you how you can make the best of your new and independent life.

The sections of this book draw together the key realities of relationship separation.

- Do not catastrophise the situation, even though tragedy is often the language used for relationship separation.
- Relationship separation and its legal and personal processes can be managed very well.
- You can manage these processes with purpose and achieve positive outcomes.

Please note that the content in this book is *not* legal advice. I will leave that to your lawyer/attorney of choice. This book is based on insights drawn from my own expertise and that of family lawyers, the expertise of professionals, research, and lessons learned from those who have experienced relationship separation.

You are not alone.

This book offers you the opportunity to proceed with resolve. I invite you to do so.

The background of abuse

All books which involve guidance are written from within a social context. The context in which this book has been forged is a very troubled one. And it is one which none of us can afford to ignore. You may be situated in it directly or feel the ripples of it throughout society; its expectations, it's normalisation, and poor government policy response which impacts all of us in one way or another. In Australia it has been referred to as a 'national emergency'. I'm speaking of *domestic abuse.*

One of the most influential contemporary commentators has been Australian journalist Jess Hill, author of *See What You Made Me Do: Power, Control and Domestic Abuse.*[1] Her compelling book lays out the context of abusive relationships.

> Domestic abuse cuts a deep wound in our society. It has been experienced by one in four Australian women. It accounts for nearly

> 60 per cent of women hospitalised for assault. It drives up to one in five female suicide attempts. Of the escalating numbers of Indigenous women in prison, 70 to 90 per cent have been a victim of family violence. From this yawning chasm comes a never-ending exodus of women and children, fleeing their homes: in 2015–16, 105,619 people – 94 per cent of them women and children – said domestic violence was the reason they'd come to a homelessness service for help.[2]
>
> Heterosexual men didn't invent abuse, and they're not the only ones to inflict it. Domestic abuse is also suffered, often in silence, by a high percentage (possibly as high as 28 per cent) of women in same-sex relationships, whose partners may convince them that if they report it they will be exiled from their community, bring shame on same-sex relationships and be laughed at by police. It's suffered by gay men, whose subordination may be secured with threats to out them, or to reveal their HIV status.[3]
>
> In this way, same-sex partner abuse is produced by the same patriarchal conditions that produce men's violence against women. It is held in place by the heterosexism and homophobia that is central to patriarchy. Ultimately, domestic abuse is a pattern of power and control, and power imbalances aren't limited to heterosexual relationships... those who perpetrate violence in same-sex relationships still do so from a position of unequal power; the greater the power difference, the more severe the physical and psychological abuse. But in heterosexual relationships, domestic abuse is also suffered by a smaller proportion of men, who, like women, stay in the vain hope they can help their abusive partners, and who may be trapped by the fear that they won't be able to protect their children if they leave.[4]

Do any of these quotes resonate with you? Please take steps to be safe if they do. And please note that *How to Save Money on Legal Fees: Separation and Divorce* refrains from dealing with the issues faced by women and children who flee for their lives or stay in domestic abuse situations. Coverage of such high conflict, lethal circumstances are best left to writers like Jess Hill and the extraordinarily dedicated service providers who help those in urgent and dangerous situations. You can find a list of these services at the end of chapter twenty.

This book is for you if you are in a situation where it is safe to leave.

The people described in Jess Hill's powerful book will not likely have the choices you have. They will not have the resources you have. Please read *How to Save Money on Legal Fees: Separation and Divorce* with awareness and purpose. Use the information as best you can in the way that is right for *you.*

How to use this book

No matter your relationship arrangement, sexual orientation, race, gender, culture or financial circumstances, this book is for you. Using this book effectively will help you make the most of the wisdom and practical solutions offered within. Throughout, I suggest practical pathways for you to consider.

Consider these approaches to the book:

- First, read the book right through in order to get a sense of its coverage. Do not worry about stopping to complete exercises or fill out forms or identify priorities. Simply go through the book in its entirety on your first read.
- Second, if urgent issues crop up for you during your first read, then make notes regarding these issues before moving on to read the book in total.
- Third, if you have not yet started your separation process, it would be wise to attend to the chapter on preparing for separation (chapter three).
- Fourth, work progressively through all chapters.
- Fifth, revisit this book as you experience the legal process of separation and communication with your family lawyer and former partner. As I stress throughout this book, *do what is right for you.*

After you have worked through this book, you will be fully prepared to provide the required documents for your lawyer. You will also better understand your priorities to drive your separation process forward and achieve your outcomes sooner rather than later.

This book offers you a learning curve. Learning about the separation process is a necessity, but you will also learn much about yourself. Appreciating the array of separation issues will offer you an awareness you may not have previously experienced.

This book is an opportunity to strengthen who you are. To be who you want to be.

Let's begin.

Dr Adrian Callum
Brisbane 2022

SECTION 1
SEPARATION

1
What is relationship separation?

The purpose of this chapter is to clarify the legal notion of separation. You may find some of the issues in this chapter confronting, but relationship separation is often a process in which you face your own realities as well as those forced upon you by the legal process.

This legal process brings into sharp relief one enduring reality: governments regulate the behaviour of citizens through laws, including relationship separation. Thus, your relationship separation brings you into the world of family law. And family law, as you will discover throughout this book, has its own rules and processes. There are ways in which you can be smart in your navigation of these rules and processes, and this book shows you how. Depending on your location in the world, the rules might vary a little.

This chapter offers you opportunities to understand:

- the overview of the legal process of separation
- what relationship separation is
- the myths surrounding separation and divorce
- the types of situations which may be regarded in legal terms as 'separation'
- the importance of resilience

The big picture of separation

The picture of Australian relationship separations is regularly provided by the Australian Bureau of Statistics. The statistical portrait tells us that in 2019, 113,815 marriages were registered in Australia and 49,116 divorces were granted. The highest divorce rate for men was for those aged between 45–49 and the highest divorce rate for women was for the ages between 40–44. Marriages lasted an average of 8.5 years before separation occurred. Overall, divorces were finalised at an average of 12.2 years after marriage.[5]

In the same year there were 5,507 same-sex marriages. Amendments to the *Marriage Act 1961* enabling same-sex couples to legally marry in Australia came into effect on 9 December 2017.[6] Female same-sex marriages outnumbered male same-sex marriages. On average, same-sex marriages occurred at an age of 36.5 years for women and 39.3 for men.

The age of people who separate and divorce has increased over time. The average age of divorce for women in Australia is 43.1 and 45.9 for men. An increasing proportion of older people are now becoming 'silver separators'. This will be discussed further in chapter three.

What do you really need to know from this number crunching? Separation is a likely aspect to coupledom. In Australia (and similar figures in other western countries), you are far from alone in separating from a partner.

Overview of the legal process

Future chapters will explore the detail of the legal process and pathways of separation and divorce. Before diving into the ways of separation discussed below, however, you should know the broad process of what will be required of you to legally complete your separation. To use Australia as an example, you (or your lawyer) can only file proceedings after you have undertaken steps to come to an agreement. Your lawyer will guide you through these steps, known as 'Pre-Action Requirements'. These include:

Pre-Action Requirements

1. Family dispute resolution
2. Exchanging a notice of intention to commence a property claim and exploring options for settlement
3. Complying with the duty of disclosure
4. Preparing a Genuine Steps Certificate outlining all the attempts made to settle the dispute

Separation

Relationship separation is one of the most important experiences you will undergo in your lifetime. Many people have mistaken assumptions about what separation is, in the legal sense. The reality is that in a number of worldwide locations, including Australia, there are several types of arrangements which may be considered 'separation' in the eyes of the Court.

I want to identify these misunderstandings and myths and provide the reality, using Australia as an example. Please make sure that you understand the realities. Inaccurate assumptions can lead to conflict, high legal costs, and bad decision-making — all of which can have awful consequences for your future.

Read carefully the following table which sets out a number of prevalent myths about relationship separation and family law. Please note especially the accurate information in response to these myths.

Myths about Separation

Myth	Reality
Everything will be divided equally	No. There is a process which involves four core considerations: • identification and valuation of the assets, liabilities and resources of the parties • the contributions of each of the parties made throughout the relationship • the future needs of each of the parties • determination of whether the proposed property settlement is just and equitable.
It wasn't my fault, therefore I'll get more.	No. There is a process which you have to follow that determines just and equitable settlement.
I need to be divorced before I can finalise my property settlement.	Wrong. Get going on your settlement upon separation.
All family law disputes must go to court.	Wrong. As few as 5% of applications actually end up in trial. People are starting to wise up to options!
The kids will live with me, so I'll be entitled to the lion's share of the assets.	No. Family law rules strictly govern the needs of the children first and foremost, and then you go from there.
The mother always gets the kids.	Not automatically. In Australia, a parent does not have legal rights over a child. Parents are expected to arrange matters in the 'best interests' of the child so that a child is free from harm and their health and welfare is ensured. Wherever appropriate, a child is expected to have a meaningful relationship with both parents.

Myth	Reality
I earned the money. She just stayed home and looked after the kids so I should get more.	Raising kids and managing multiple demands of creating and maintaining a home and 'family' contributes to the combined income of the household, whatever job you do. The law indicates direct and indirect financial contributions to the relationship (which come in many forms) determine the property settlement.
We had a long marriage. It's a straight 50–50 split.	There is no 50–50 rule in Australia.
We have now separated so they can't get my inheritance.	Not necessarily. Get your settlement finalised and legally binding *before* you receive your inheritance.
My Ex has a well-paid job, so I'm entitled to spousal maintenance.	This is not automatic. Depends on personal circumstances. Court typically expects you to earn an income of your own. Exceptional circumstances include physical/mental disability.
We're not married so the law is different for us (de facto relationships).	Family law is the same for all relationships, including same-sex, de facto and marriage. Factors considered for de facto: • how long you have been in the relationship • whether a sexual relationship exists • degree of financial independence, interdependence, arrangements for financial support • whether you own property together.
I can keep property after a divorce by placing the title in someone else's name.	Exchanging titles, arranging for assets to be returned to you once the property settlement is finalised or failing to provide 'full and frank' disclosure regarding assets in order to avoid its inclusion in the property settlement may be considered fraud by the Court and result in you receiving less of the property pool.

How many of these myths have you believed up until now? It's worth remembering that many of the myths surrounding relationship separation have been driven by a lack of research, bigotry, resentment towards lawyers and the family law process, sheer self-interest, and gender bias.

Let's take a brief look at the issue of gender.

In a heterosexual-based assessment supported by many respected financial consultancy firms, The Australian Institute of Family Studies confirms:

> that women are more likely to feel the financial impacts of a divorce, with some straightforward reasons for this. In many (though not all) separations, it is the woman who becomes the primary caregiver for children. This can make it more challenging for women to pursue a career, and many opt for part-time work, which can also see their superannuation savings take a hit. Men, on the other hand, may have more time to devote to their career and this can mean greater income-earning potential; however they also have child support to deal with.[7]

That said, not all men pay child support. This has long been the case.[8] Furthermore, women are often reluctant to pursue child support from fathers for risk of violence to themselves and their children. The option is open for women to talk to their family lawyer to secure financial support from the father.

Another respected organisation, Relationships Australia, has observed the gendered differences of separation. How many of these feelings resonate with you as a woman? As a man?

Women have reported a range of intense feelings at various stages of separation including feeling:

- scared about the responsibility for their economic future and that of their children
- sad about the break-up of the family unit
- nervous about how they will juggle work and home commitments

- resentful about career sacrifices they may have made in their role of homemaker
- hateful towards their former partner
- bitter about their new circumstances
- worried about dealing with bureaucracies and the legal system
- fearful of making the same mistakes in another relationship
- concerned that the relationship with the former partner may remain in conflict
- relief that things are out in the open.[9]

The list below are examples of feelings that men have reported to Relationships Australia:

- frustration, powerless, and anger
- relief that differences are out in the open
- dizziness, with thoughts spinning in circles
- desperation, ready to drop off the planet
- determination to stand ground and battle to the bitter end
- awareness of some hard choices having to be made
- loneliness and sadness
- shock, bewilderment, and hurt.[10]

How many of these have you experienced lately? While these are socio-psychological impacts, there are also medical impacts for men and women who experience separation. High conflict is obviously perilous to your health. Medicos declare that many people experience depression, anxiety, grief, anger, and/or irritability. People also may experience pronounced mental and physical fatigue. The abuse of alcohol, prescription drugs and illegal substances, overeating and smoking tend to emerge as coping mechanisms in response to issues ignited by separation.

I cannot stress enough that the end of your relationship is *not* the end of the world. There is a future beyond tomorrow. The reality is, separation is *not* always painful. *Separation can be a fruitful experience.* Ask yourself, 'What positive outcomes can result from my separation?'. This applies whether you leave or your partner leaves the relationship.

Be wary of the language of tragedy and try not to catastrophise your situation. It may be that you're putting your health at risk. Keep your eye on the future.

What does 'separation' mean?

Many a family law textbook declares 'separation' as the acknowledged ending of a marital or de facto relationship (now inclusive of a same-sex relationship) with no viable prospect of reconciliation.

Separation can occur in a number of different ways in the eyes of the Court. Whichever way you choose to separate try to ensure that you let family, friends, Medicare, Centrelink, child support agencies and schools know about your situation. Don't forget to notify your bank, insurance and superannuation companies. The manner of your separation may require proof. If your situation involves you leaving home take key items with you. For example: personal identification, passport, credit and debit cards, bank details, financial statements, tax returns, marriage certicate, and items you and your children need. While these ways of separation might vary according to the state/country you live in, using the Australian situation as an illustration may assist you in appreciating the complexity of the legal definition of 'separation'.

According to the *Family Law Act 1975 (Cth)* the forms of arrangements listed below are recognised as 'separation'.[11]

Types of Legally Recognised Separation in Australia

Trial separation	'Give it a go and see how you feel'. Court will accommodate this in your separation.
Separation under one roof	Increasingly common. Low conflict but not without conflict. Done to reduce financial loss. Often done for sake of the kids.
Mutual decision to end the relationship	Not always without conflict.
Your partner leaves you	Get some support.
One partner leaves	Best done after seeking lawyer's advice.
Court-ordered separation	Court orders one party to leave home. Court perceives other parties in the home to be at risk.

Making sure that you have the correct legal understanding of separation will influence the money-saving and time-saving efficiency with which you prepare for your separation. The actions and practicalities of preparing for separation are discussed in chapter three. If your situation allows for preparation use the steps suggested which are relevant to your circumstances.

Social change can make a noticeable difference to the choices you make in the circumstances of your separation. This book, for instance, was finalised in the COVID-19 pandemic. Sustained lockdowns meant that couples were compelled to spend extended periods of time together at home. For many couples this became intolerable. Family lawyers were besieged by inquiries about separation, what it involved, and how to do it. Moreover, the financial pressure on couples and families heralded a change in the circumstances of separation. With family budgets on the line in the face of mass job losses, financial and domestic abuse skyrocketed. Financial pressure led to an increase in the 'living under one roof' model of separation. 'Togetherness' has brought 'separateness' into sharp relief.

Three key factors essential to your separation success

What is a 'successful separation'? Success may mean many things to many people. *At its core, the key to separation success is minimised legal costs, effective lawyer advice, timely progress, low conflict, and outcomes that allow you to get on with your life.* Any successful separation will result in a positive transformation for you. There is a consensus amongst family law clients and lawyers that three key factors are essential to your separation success. Let's look at them now.

Factor 1: Your choice of lawyer

Your choice of lawyer plays a crucial role in minimising your legal spend. Issues such as the quality of legal advice, legal skill, communication and negotiation skill, cultural awareness, and sheer savvy can fuel successful outcomes. 'Savvy' is the agility of your lawyer to be across a number of the areas presented by you, the client. Savvy lawyers have a thorough understanding of your separation situation, comprehensive understanding of coercive control, financial insight, and problem-solving skills. Although you are paying your lawyer for their legal services, savvy lawyers manage the client-lawyer relationship as teamwork. Your choice of lawyer will make all the difference.

Factor 2: How you use the services of your lawyer

There has been a change in client expectations of lawyers in recent years. Expectations of greater billing transparency and client self-education (emerging from the consumerist and self-help movements) have coincided with increasing public revelations of poor lawyer behaviour. This has resulted in formal complaints by clients to regulatory bodies alleging either unsatisfactory conduct or professional misconduct.[12]

If you are someone who does not trust the legal profession, why not use your mistrust to fuel your resolve to find the best family lawyer available to you? Fuel your commitment to take responsibility for your separation process. Take charge rather than passively letting your lawyer run the show.

Resolve to turn your problems into solutions. Learn what is required of you. If you need your lawyer to go in and bat for you, be sure to let them. Doing this does *not* compromise your sense of purpose. Make smart decisions on sound advice (and not emotion) to achieve favourable outcomes.

Factor 3: Low conflict or high conflict

Your behaviour and/or the behaviour of your Ex can make things far more difficult than necessary. It only takes one partner to make matters a nightmare for all concerned, including your children, other family members, close friends, and even the lawyers involved. To be frank, lawyers warm neither to high-conflict clients and their reckless escalation of legal costs, nor the destruction to others they cause. If you or your Ex are quick to temper, aggressive or abusive, this limits your options and drains the funds you will need for your future.

Do you need to spend all of your money on legal fees to enact revenge? Fight for a possession that may mean little in the long run? Acknowledgement that you are right? Or are you just being vindictive? Manage your anger and manage your responses to the anger expressed by your Ex as best you can. *How* you handle your conflict with your Ex matters. Wherever possible, communicating for outcomes will help you achieve a successful separation.

INSIGHT: How to strengthen your resilience

How much change can you tolerate?

The varying ability of people to cope with change has been the subject of much research by psychologists and sociologists. Mess will dominate your life if you fail to reach out for help to cope with life changes with which you struggle. Relationship separation is a major change in a person's life, whether you leave or you are the one who has been left.

Think about times in your life when you have had to adjust to change, when life did not go your way. What attitude did you adopt? What actions did you take to deal with this change? Can you apply these attitudes and actions to your separation? How well you cope with change can influence how much money you spend on legal fees. For instance, if you do not cope well with change generally, and delay or avoid completing necessary tasks, this will cost you money.

Ask for help. If your anxiety and confusion paralyses you and you do not ask for help and achieve short-term relief by handing everything over to your lawyer, this too will cost you. Failing to self manage any mess in your life will not end in positive outcomes.

Ironically, throwing yourself into achieving favourable outcomes from your separation process will transform you anyway. You may not notice these changes at first. Or you might feel the slow thrill of growing confidence.

How do *you* cope with change and hardship? The term 'resilience' is often used to talk about coping with change. So what does 'resilience' really mean? Many psychologists describe resilience as 'the ability to adapt in the face of adversity, significant stress or trauma'.[13] Resilience can be *learned* since it involves thoughts, attitudes, behaviours and actions which you can develop to cope with significant stress in your life. Being 'resilient' does not mean that you do not experience distress or fear or anxiety or sadness. You do.

But the good news is that not only can you learn resilience and develop it, you can keep getting better at it. Psychological experts suggest that resilience results from a combination of factors. It is influenced by caring and supportive relationships within the family and outside of it. Relationships that provide trust, positive role models, reassurance and encouragement are ones which also foster resilience.

The following four factors are strongly associated with resilience:

1. the capacity to make realistic plans and carry them out
2. a positive view of oneself and confidence in one's abilities
3. skills in communication and problem solving
4. the capacity to manage strong feelings and impulses.[14]

It is easy to see how the end of a relationship can undermine these capacities. Learning resilience is an individual and personal endeavour. The key to learning resilience skills is fidelity—a commitment to your self-development based on what works for you.

You can foster your resilience. I have adapted the following ten resilience tips provided by the American Psychological Association to the issue of relationship separation. You may find some of them more useful than others. Can you apply one or more of these strategies to grow your own resilience?

1. Accept that change is part of living

Your separation may have been unexpected and will mostly likely require arrangements that need to be completed quickly, such as alternative accommodation, parenting rearrangements, and sourcing or rearranging financial resources. Do you find making unexpected arrangements stressful? If you have the choice to *prepare* for separation, do so. Heeding the advice in chapter three can make your life much easier.

Imposed changes in self-perception and identity can be disorienting. Significant life-changing events means that you no longer see the world, or yourself, in the same way. When you accept that your relationship is over and identify the changes that need to be made, you can focus on how best to make those changes to suit your future.

2. Avoid seeing crises as insurmountable problems

This is easy to say and hard to do. Problems *do* seem insurmountable when you are in the throes of intense emotion, whether it be guilt, anger, hurt or abandonment. Unexpected separation, especially, can invite overwhelm to the point where you cannot think clearly.

But problems *can* be solved. You know this because you will have solved problems prior to your separation. That's called life experience! *You* are in control of choosing how you understand and respond to the ending of your relationship. Even getting help from a psychologist to address issues which challenge you, is you taking control of life-changing events and their effects.

3. Take decisive actions

Make decisions and take actions to deal with your separation (for more on decision-making see chapter four). Create a timeline by which certain actions need to be completed. This can be so empowering. When you take action in the face of adversity, you take control. You will feel good about yourself. And you will feel the momentum of progress. You can achieve a sense that the crisis can be managed—that *you can* manage.

4. Keep things in perspective

The end of your relationship is *not the end of the world,* though it may seem like it at the time. You are not dead. Your children are not dead. Your closest friends will stick by you. The universe has not come to a standstill. Shopping still needs to be done. People will still smile and wave to you. Your dog will want breakfast. Washing needs to be done. You still have to attend to daily living tasks. Sure, you feel bad. *But you will get through this.*

Try the resilience exercise of listing all of the reasons why the end of your relationship is *not* the end of the world. How many reasons can you list? Can you add a column to this list and every day identify things you can do now that you are single? Things which you could not do before? Can you see now how the process of building your resilience is such a personal one? When you get a better sense of *how* the end of your relationship reshapes your life after listing the decisions and actions required, your sense of control will keep growing and help you maintain a healthy and realistic perspective.

5. Take care of yourself

Coping with adversity and making smart decisions is easier if you attend to your health needs. Try to eat well, exercise, get enough sleep and do activities that you find pleasurable or satisfying, even if it is just a walk in the park or getting lost in the crowd. Take care of yourself and make sure that you look after your health. Self-care *fuels your ability to focus and think clearly*. Steer clear of comfort food and junk food. Instant satisfaction through bad food is not sustainable. The benefits of taking good care of yourself during separation include saving money!

6. Make connections

Few benefit from going through a separation on their own. Be sure to draw on your network of friends and family for comfort and emotional sustenance. Talk through your issues with a trusted friend, family member or a professional. Interacting with people may be the very last thing some of you feel like doing when you are in emotional pain, but the same rule applies as when fighting depression—make your bed, clean your home, get active and make connections with people. There is a saying which goes, 'Get up, get dressed, and get out'. Even if you do not want to engage, an activity like volunteering can improve your sense of self-worth. You can meet people who do not know about your situation and you can keep busy. And you might even find meeting other volunteers refreshing. Separation does not mean that you cannot feel good about yourself. *Participate*. Cease avoiding. If you need help to make social connections, ask for it. Support will be there for you. See chapter twenty for more information on how to find help.

7. Move toward your goals

Why not have a 'win'? Try to achieve something that you did not manage yesterday. This might be doing more exercise, eating healthily, attending a social engagement or developing a friendship. How you go about your goals has to be what suits *you and your situation*. Set yourself small and achievable challenges so that you can succeed and build your self-esteem at your own pace. List your goals. The act of writing them down and thinking them through actually helps you get stronger. Take regular action to move closer to these goals. Progress might seem slow at first, but make a start. Taking that first step can feel so good. Move in the direction you want to go and you will soon find that your pace picks up. Achieving goals fortifies motivation. Good things can happen because *you make them happen.*

8. Nurture a positive view of yourself

The minefield of separation can be powerful in undermining your self-perception, so nurturing a positive view of yourself takes determination and practice. Go through the exercise of describing yourself. Write it down. Read it out aloud. Does this sound reasonable or unduly negative? Now write down a description of who you want to be. What kind of qualities do you wish you had? Write these qualities down. Now work on building them. With time, the amount of effort this takes will start to go unnoticed. It may be that it will become like driving: automatic.

9. Maintain a hopeful outlook

Visualising yourself achieving your goals is one way to remain optimistic about your life. Understand what you fear and why. List your fears and why you have them. What is the worst thing that can happen? Do not let your fear paralyse you. Deliberately develop a positive outlook by practising optimism. Focus on the positive aspects of your life and achieving a goal every single day.

10. Look for opportunities for self-discovery

If nothing else, a life-changing event like separation will position you to discover much about yourself and help you to gain insightful self-knowledge. Doing this is empowering. Being no longer burdened will not only make a positive difference to you but those around you. What do you have to lose?

Conclusion

This list of suggestions for strengthening your resilience is not exhaustive. Actively exercising your resilience skills will help you think clearly about matters which demand your consideration. It will also help you minimise the amount of money you spend on your legal fees.

Having considered the legal notion of 'separation' under Australian law, let's move on to the practicalities of property division and how you can save money in doing so.

2

Who gets what? Division of property

How do you divide fairly the property amassed by you and your Ex once your relationship has ended? Who gets what? What's fair? Are future needs taken into account? Is earning capacity relevant? The purpose of this chapter is to foster your understanding of the legal function and process of your property settlement. Once you understand how property settlement works, your decision-making will be smarter (especially if you get financial advice beforehand) and you will start to make major contributions to your bank of skills, knowledge and abilities — all of which will save you money.

This chapter offers you opportunities to understand:

- the notion of 'property'
- ideas within the process of property division
- the process of property division itself
- the core legal principles of property division

Consent orders

It is important to understand that your property settlement will not be finalised until it is formalised by the Court. In Australia, there is now a greater expectation on parties to demonstrate genuine attempts to come to an agreement regarding the division of assets prior to applying to the Court for proposed Consent Orders. You will need to provide a Genuine Steps Certificate along with your first and hopefully final filing of proposed Consent Orders to the Court.

This term, 'proposed Consent Orders', refers to the forms which are submitted to the Court so that the settlement reached between you and your Ex can be assessed as 'just and equitable'. If they are deemed 'just and equitable' your proposed Consent Orders will be approved by the Court. The term, 'just and equitable' is the Court's distribution to you and your Ex of assets after a four-step process, discussed below, is conducted to evaluate the assets and debts accrued by you and your Ex during your relationship.

Take care with this. Automatic approval of your application for proposed Consent Orders is not guaranteed. The Court has a duty to ensure that the details of the agreement which comprise your proposed Consent Orders amount to a settlement which is 'just and equitable' to both parties. Details must be accurate, forms must be completed correctly, full disclosure must be evident.

In short, every 't' must be crossed and every 'i' must be dotted. Any mistakes and your proposed Consent Orders will be returned. This will delay your process and become expensive.

Timing

All separation management tasks take time. Start as soon as you can. Note the date of your relationship separation. The reasons for this are driven by timelines set by the Court. There are time limits to apply for proposed Consent Orders. You must apply within one year from the date your Divorce Order has taken effect and within two years from the date your de facto relationship ended. Whether de facto or married, do not assume the Court will approve your proposed Consent Orders should you exceed the due date.

Time matters for another reason. Until you legally finalise your separation, your Ex has the right to claim part of your finances and assets. This includes inheritance, large contracts in your family business and so on. So, get to the point of proposed Consent Orders as soon as you can.

One thing you absolutely must get straight from the get-go. When dealing with the legal profession and the Court, rules are rules!

What does 'property' mean?

Having discussed two important aspects of property settlement, it's time to make sure that you understand what is meant by the term 'property' in family law. Many people who embark on separation are often surprised at the inclusiveness of the term. For instance, many are shocked to learn that family pets (discussed in chapter fifteen) are considered 'property'.

The assessment of the 'property pool' refers to the evaluation of assets and liabilities. Sounds simple, doesn't it? But there is much more to the story. The notion of 'property', in the legal sense, includes houses, cars, household contents, family-run businesses, investment properties, farm animals, family pets, superannuation, and, depending on your age, pensions/retirement funds.

It is essential for you to remember that whether property is held in your name, your Ex's, or both names, all of this property goes into the 'property pool' to be divided between you and your former spouse.

The four-step process of property division

Now that you are clear about what 'property' actually means in family law, let's look at the four-step process of property division to ensure that your settlement is 'just and equitable'.

The four steps of property division:

1. Determine your combined net worth
2. Assess each person's contribution to the pool of wealth
3. Identify the individual needs of each party
4. Start negotiating

Each of these steps merit explanation to understand them better.

1. Determine your combined net worth

This is an obvious starting point since any evaluation of liabilities and assets has to begin with listing all of your assets and liabilities in a document.[15]

This document is not only essential for your lawyer, but it will also form the starting point for any discussions or negotiations. The term 'net worth' refers to assets minus liabilities. Net worth is what is owned minus what is owed. The value of assets is determined at the date of separation. However, if your matter ends up in Court, the value will be determined as that at the time of commencement of Court proceedings.

While some of you may consider going to Court an unlikely event, this guidance regarding value can matter a great deal. For instance, property prices, like share portfolios, can rise and fall quickly. Conducting a cost ratio against legal fees might be advisable here, since legal fees will mount while protracted negotiations regarding settlement ensue. Once you list what you owe and what you own, you are then in a position to identify your accrued net worth and conduct your cost ratios. Do not forget to consult your government website about the property division process.

You may require the assistance of an experienced valuer to help you arrive at the figure of net worth. Rather than have your lawyer organise the valuations, think about doing as much of this as you can yourself.

There are websites that provide market value on vehicles based on relevant details such as the make, model and condition of your vehicle. Consider printing this information out and including it in your settlement information. While this is not a valuation of your own vehicle, it is a useful guide to arriving at an accepted price, what lawyers refer to as 'the midpoint' for the private sale figure for your vehicle.

If possible, try to agree with your Ex on the one independent valuer. This will prevent disagreement about the valuation determined and the possibility of one partner over- or under-valuing assets to gain advantage. Take care with your expenditures on valuers of specific types, such as forensic accountants, and other specialists, because these services can be very expensive (which is one reason why your family lawyer should be finance savvy). If you can, conduct your own research regarding the value of particular items. Chapter six will deal with disclosure and deceit to assist your judgement.

Remember this: be realistic, honest and accurate when assessing the value of assets and liabilities to accurately identify your net worth.

2. Assess each person's contribution to the pool of wealth

It is generally agreed that your combined 'asset pool' stems from four sources.

The first is your financial contribution to the relationship. Financial contributions include earned income by each party, redundancy payments, inheritances, who owns the family home, and so on.

The second type of contribution to the combined asset pool is parenting. This includes time dedicated to raising the children. It is often women who surrender their career to raise children. While the economic significance of parenting is often ridiculed in comments by the uninformed, parenting is a very significant contribution because it frees up the other partner to seek income and enjoy flexibility. This puts pressure on the primary parent's fixed responsibilities which limits their flexibility and earning capacity.

The third type of contribution to the combined asset pool is homemaking; the recognised credit to the person's contribution of running the household. Australia's most eminent financial adviser, Paul Clitheroe, has argued that parenting and homemaking contributions 'should reassure anyone who was a non-working parent that they're still entitled to a decent stake of the marital assets even if they weren't a breadwinner bringing a wage or salary into the household'.[16]

The fourth type of contribution to the combined asset pool are those deemed to be non-financial, beyond those of parenting and homemaking. Non-financial contributions include partners caring for parents as well as children, assisting in the family business, doing up a partner's sole trader accounts, acting as receptionist for a partner's business, and other administration and purchasing duties. Or one partner may have dedicated their time and effort to renovating an investment property in order to improve its value, or simply renovated the family home to improve its real estate value in the future.[17] Non-financial contributions can vary.

3. Identify the individual needs of each party

The current and future needs of both parties will be considered by the Court in order to determine the division of property. There are many factors taken into account when considering individual needs. Some factors include:

- the age and state of health of you and your Ex
- the income, property and financial resources of you and your Ex
- your physical and mental capacity for appropriate future employment
- whether either of you has the care and control of children aged under 18
- the responsibilities of either of you to support any other person
- your eligibility for a Centrelink pension (Australia) or other support payment depending on the state/country in which you live
- the duration of your relationship (the longer your relationship, the less weight the initial individual financial contributions are likely to carry).[18]

4. Start negotiating

The fourth and final step in the property division process can also be the most sensitive part. If you are in a position to do so, please seriously consider getting financial advice to support your decision-making. Act to prevent financial regret.

Whatever option you choose for legally finalising your separation, the bargaining over property items will be a necessary aspect of your process. Bargaining is where you and your Ex identify what the other wants, what the other will not concede, and where both of you make concessions.

It's not unusual for this stage to be highly provocative. Be sure to read chapter four on decision-making and anger. It is also important for you to note that this stage is not always volatile. There *are* reasonable settlements, despite the myths and horror stories which abound. Remember, most people *do* achieve settlement and many of them are amicable.

Conflict is never compulsory.

In the coming chapters you will encounter ways of communicating with your Ex to prevent conflict and unnecessary expense.

Insight: Household contents

Make an inventory of all household items. You're welcome to use the sample template at the end of this chapter (remember, a full template can be found on my author website). Complete it as thoroughly as you can and with as much detail as possible. Do not forget locations like the garage, loft/attic, the yard, or pool equipment. Creating categories for household furniture can help keep you organised. For instance, consider categories like vehicles, furnishings, furniture, appliances, kitchenware, linen, antiques, collectibles, sports equipment, tools and other garage items.

List *all* major items, including heirlooms and jewellery. If you have items securely stored elsewhere, make sure you list them too. Have a safety deposit box full of valuables? List them! Everyone has contents that are especially important to them. They may be photo albums of when the children were growing up, portraits of family ancestors, a precious item given to you by your mother, and so on. Do you know which items are special to your former partner? Are there non-marital assets (assets brought into the marriage) you have forgotten? Catalogue everything, especially if the other party knows that it would hurt you not to have them and is the kind of person who would use that against you. Do not forget your small items when large items are staring you in the face. List your small devices, mobile phones and tablets, paintings, dinnerware, and children's toys.

Some lawyers will informally advise you to remove your most precious items *now*, before you leave, and put them somewhere safe until you relocate so they cannot be used against you as leverage. This is for *you* to decide. If you choose to do this, make sure you inform your lawyer and include it in your asset disclosure.

If your Ex has password protected files to which you do not have access, try to take photographs of the hard drive so that you can apply for access should your former partner prove hostile and uncooperative. If you do not have this level of computer skill, enlist the help of a trusted friend who does, or hire a company which specialises in this service—and do it quickly.

Once you leave you may not be in a position to control access to your precious items or information that you need.

Now go ahead and photograph every item on your list. It is in your interest to document and photograph every item, and keep a list of those items you have not photographed. Your set of photographs should match your list of items as much as possible. Remember, detail and organisation are powerful allies, no matter what your situation.

You will recall that earlier I mentioned that determining your property settlement will require valuation information regarding house, vehicle, and/ or business. Household contents also require valuation.

Do as much of your household valuation as you can. It is time-consuming but it will save you money and keep you aware of what possessions you have.

Household contents such as furniture and whitegoods (excluding antiques and collectibles) are valued not on insurance value, as many mistakenly think, but on *secondhand dealer value*. Remember this because it can be an expensive exercise purchasing new items.

After you have completed this inventory and sourced the required financial information, save a copy of this information and pass it on to your lawyer.

This preparation will ensure that you are across the financial aspects of the property to be divided and be in a stronger bargaining position. It will make you less susceptible to deceit. It will also save you money.

Household Inventory

Item	Purchase Price	2nd Hand Price	Possession You / Ex	Source (How item was acquired)

Conclusion

Preparing for your property division requires detailed time-consuming work on your part. But it is worth it. The effort and care you put into this task will be powerful in helping you be organised, fully across your assets and liabilities, and position you to decide what you want to keep and what you are prepared to release. Thorough preparation toughens your resolve. It boosts your sense of control. And it saves you money.

Now that you have the steps of property division under your belt, let's now turn to the fundamental issues of separation preparation and its importance to reducing your spending on legal fees.

Financial Profile

Bank Accounts

- Name and address of banks
- Names on the account/s
- Account number/s
- Type of account/s
- Date/s account was opened
- Current balance/s

Education

This section is relevant only if you are providing your former partner with an education, or your former spouse is providing you with an education. Provide background details if you worked whilst your former partner was gaining an education.

- Which partner gained the education
- Dates of education duration
- Type of education
- Your annual salary while your former partner was gaining an education
- Source of your income
- Annual salary of former partner if s/he worked
- Source of income to your former partner
- Superannuation payments
- Lost superannuation contributions/benefit
- Details of other income to you or your former partner

Insurance and superannuation

Write down the following information for each insurance policy you have. If you know there are other insurance policies but do not have access to them, then be sure to notify your lawyer. If you have more than one insurance policy, be sure to complete a separate page and to use the detail required (listed below).

- Name of insurance company/ies
- Type of policy/ies, e.g. life insurance
- Policy number/s
- Name of person/s insured
- Name of beneficiary/ies
- Face value of the policy/ies
- Cash value of the policy/ies
- Outstanding loans against the policy/ies
- Amount/s outstanding
- Any premiums payable (monthly/yearly)

Retirement plan or pension fund

If you have more than one retirement plan or pension fund, be sure to complete a separate page and to use the detail required (listed below). Ask your accountant to prepare this information.

- Name of plan
- Contributions to plan
- Co-contributions to plan
- Current collectible lump sum

Business and trusts

If you own an interest in a business, or your former spouse or you have trusts, provide details below. Ask your accountant to prepare this information.

- Date of marriage/life partnership
- Date business interest was acquired
- Name of business
- Date business commenced
- Type of business
- Is the business incorporated
- Names of directors
- If a public business, total number of shares
- Number of shares in your name
- Number of shares in the name of your former partner
- Name of any other stakeholders (e.g. trusts)
- Number of employees
- Value of assets
- Profit or loss business made in the last three years
- Profit or loss business made last tax quarter
- Location of business accounts books
- Name of person who runs the business
- Last three years of tax returns
- Details of trust/s, e.g. name of trust, trustee, beneficiaries, assets owned

Real estate

This section permits details for one item of real estate. Be sure to complete separate pages for other items of real estate and to use the detail requested here.

- Names on title/legal ownership
- Type of real estate
- Address
- Date of purchase
- Purchase price
- Deposit amount
- Source of deposit
- If outstanding loan, amount of monthly payments
- To whom payments are made and how they are made
- Amount of taxes paid (if investment only)
- Are insurances currently up to date
- Current mortgage balance
- Current market value of property, e.g. real estate appraisal (these need to be formally valued and documented by the relevant valuer).

Separate property or property contributed to the relationship

Provide details regarding separate property which is distinct from the real estate issue above. Separate property refers to property owned by you or your former partner that was brought into the relationship/partnership, inherited during the relationship/partnership, or purchased with funds from the sale of other separate property. If you have more than one separate property item, be sure to complete a separate page and to use the detail required (listed below).

- Type of property
- Date property was acquired
- How the property was acquired
- Price paid for the property
- Payments made during relationship/partnership
- Market value of the property
- Amount owed on the property
- Name of creditor
- Details of inheritance funds, e.g. when it was received, from where, and for whose benefit

Investments other than real property

This section requires details of the types of investments you and your former partner may currently possess. Complete details on a separate page for investments such as stocks, bonds, mutual funds, etc. Be sure to include details which include:

- Name
- Account ID
- Purchase price
- Market value
- Current total
- Certificates of Deposit
- Maturity date
- Location of Certificates of Deposit
- Interest
- If investments are managed by a financial advisor, provide contact details

Vehicles

Write down the detail of any vehicles owned. These may include your cars, recreational vehicles, motorcycles, or farming vehicles. If you have more than one vehicle, be sure to complete a separate page and to use the detail required (listed below).

- Type of vehicle
- Licence number of vehicle
- Make of vehicle
- Model of vehicle
- Year of manufacture
- Balance owed on vehicle
- Market value of vehicle
- Name of registered vehicle owner

3
Separation preparation saves money

Planning your separation can help you manage the challenging psychological issues that can emerge during this period of intense change. Planning, reading and researching, talking to experts, reorganising your finances, thinking through the arrangements for your children's care and schooling, listing household items, and attending to your employment arrangements are all tasks to complete in a timely fashion. Completing these tasks as soon as you feel able can save you money and begin the precious process of preparing yourself to reshape your life.

This chapter offers you opportunities to understand:

- the steps you can take to save money in your separation preparation
- considerations for 'silver separators'
- the basics of budgeting

Preparing for separation

The separation preparation steps discussed in this book can help you forge a more efficient environment in which to complete tasks required to legally formalise the end of your relationship. While every separation is different, be sure to note down points that apply to you, whether you separate in your younger or older years.

Earlier, I mentioned that data from the Australian Bureau of Statistics indicated that your forties are when the light bulb moment for separation decisions occur.[19] This pattern is changing. More couples above the age of forty are taking this decision. There are signs that the proportion of people aged in their fifties and sixties leaving their relationships is increasing, with women mostly initiating the separation.[20]

This increase is similar to the United Kingdom and the United States. For instance, in the United States, one in four divorces is among people who are aged over fifty. There are factors other than longer life expectancy which contribute to this change. These include increased women's participation in the paid labour force, the erosion of the stigma attached to divorce, intolerance to serial infidelities, poor communication, and the need for self-fulfillment. Baby boomers who decide to go their separate ways are now described as 'silver separators' who decide on 'grey divorce'.

If you are a 'silver separator' other factors will also demand your consideration. Greater attention to health and medical issues, and protection of retirement funds is essential. If you are in this age group and separating, it is essential that you do not waste money on legal fees. You need to be astute with your decisions. Consider your vision for your retirement. Do you now need to change it? For instance, do you now need to ensure that your aged care is funded adequately? What about your estate planning?

Separation for older people tends to be a time-sensitive matter. Time spent in a relationship in which damage has occurred means time needs to be spent *recovering* when there is not a lot of time left to build a new life. Spending time on a protracted legal process should *not* be part of this. Astute decisions need to be made in terms of the big picture of time and the sharp picture of finances. Neither time nor finances should be squandered.

Whatever your age, the suggestions listed below can help ease the way for you. This list is divided into two categories: general preparation and financial preparation.

General preparation

Safety

How and when you leave matters. You will find a list of support services and emergency help at the end of chapter twenty that may assist you.

Your safety is paramount. If you have children their safety is also crucial. For women, the point of *leaving* has a long history of being the most dangerous moment in the process of separation. If your circumstances permit you to plan and prepare, then absolutely do so. If your relationship with your former partner has been abusive—physically, psychologically or financially—then it is essential that you take this into account in your planning. There are numerous ways to ensure your safety, if you are in a situation which allows this. I say this, knowing full well that many leave during a crisis point, no matter the type of relationship you are in. Some escape during the acts of violence and seek help from a refuge, some need to leave with help of police. Be safe. Ask for help if you can.

Contact details

Changing your email address is an important part of your preparation. You need to control who has communication access to you. Couples often share the one email address. If you and your Ex have shared the one email address create a new email address and secure password for yourself *immediately*. Be smart with your password and use a mix of numbers and letters your former partner will never guess — keep a copy of your password somewhere safe.

Be sure to copy all of the contacts in your joint email contact list so you do not lose contact with people who matter to you. Use your new email address to notify your most trusted friends of your new contact details. Word your emails with care. Keep your email short, to the point, and simple. Your purpose is simply to notify people of the change in your circumstances. Be sure to tell them this change in contact details is to protect your safety/privacy and should not be shared with anyone. Notify key service providers and finance/insurance providers. For instance, ask your doctor, your children's school, your accountant, as well as other key service providers, not to disclose your contact details.

For example, consider an email like this:

> *Dear* ______________
>
> *This is to let you know that* _____ *and I have separated. Please note the new email address for contacting me. These new contact details are confidential. It is essential that you do not pass on my contact details.*
>
> *Thank you,*
>
> ____________________

Opening a new post box is also a good idea. If you have opened a post box for a new postal address, be sure to notify the people who matter to you. It is a relatively straightforward process to organise redirection of your mail *prior* to leaving so that all of your mail is forwarded to your new post box. Whatever you do, avoid sharing details about your new situation using social media. We live in a digital time. Your Ex will find out quickly if you blast your news over social media. Beginning the process which leads to you starting life afresh requires your care at each and every step of the way.

Learn your legal rights and obligations

Get cracking on learning about your legal rights and responsibilities to prevent yourself from making costly mistakes. Your first point of call may well be checking key websites such as your government's Court/Family Law website. For instance, the Australian government has a useful website fcfcoa.gov.au. This site contains fact sheets and information on processes for different types of family law circumstances. Wherever you reside outside of Australia there will be a similar website. Please make sure you read it carefully and write down any questions or issues you do not understand for discussion with your lawyer.

You could also consult the website of your local Law Society. All lawyers belong to a Law Society. Law Societies have websites which serve the community as well as their members. Members of the community can access resources such as fact sheets and links to professionals relevant to their local state or county. I can tell you from personal experience that Law Societies are staffed with knowledgeable specialists who provide excellent customer service.

Ultimately, consulting a lawyer is the smartest step to learn about your rights and responsibilities, options and decisions (see section four for legal pathways). Treat this relationship as a project management, business-like relationship where you go having done research of your own (if you can) and prepared with a list of questions.

Stay focused on getting the information you need. Leave your emotions out of this equation. Understand that all your family lawyer will be interested in are the facts of your particular situation. They will use their legal skills to help you achieve your goals. While your lawyer will acknowledge that you are understandably upset, vent your distress when you see your friends, family or a psychologist.

Dealing with your emotions is not the service for which you are paying your lawyer.

Sure, you want your lawyer to endorse your opinion that you have been hard done by, treated unfairly and deserve vigorous representation—you want to be heard and you want to be affirmed. Here is the reality: your lawyer is *obliged* to provide you with the best representation anyway.

Consulting a lawyer is crucial, even if you plan to do some of the process work yourself. By consulting your lawyer you will have an information base upon which you can make smart decisions for handling your key separation tasks. For instance, if you are leaving, do not vacate your house until you are in possession of all of the necessary legal advice and information. Making uninformed decisions based upon the experience of a friend, neighbour, or workmate is *not* smart. *Everyone's situation is different.* Poor decision-making can cost you a lot of money and damage relationships you value. What's more, poor decisions can have consequences that are serious and long-lasting (see chapter four). So, please consult a trustworthy family lawyer before doing anything. How to do this will be discussed in section five.

Keep a personal file

Keep a personal file which contains original documentation (as opposed to copies) of details about you, and if children are involved, your children. Documents which should be included in your file would be your birth certificate, and those of your children, your marriage certificate (if you have one), your citizenship certificate, bank account details, financial records (such as bank statements and tax returns), superannuation, and insurance policies. Do this while you can readily access them. You will need these for your new and independent life.[21] In his latest book, *The Barefoot Investor for Families*, Scott Pape recommends that people create a 'Fearless Folder' containing such documents and purchase a fireproof and waterproof safe in which to keep them secure.[22]

Support network

Separation and divorce will not leave you untouched. There are myriad emotions that accompany separation and divorce. These emotions can be complex and conflicting. They will very likely jeopardise your decision-making across a whole range of areas in your life, so put in place a support network to get you through the tough times. These good people can act as a sounding board for your decisions. They can share outings with you. They can help with chores around the house. They can listen to you when you need to unburden yourself. They can mind the children. They can help with shopping. They can show you that you are not alone. They can help you in all sorts of ways. They will make an important difference to how you cope in the long run.

Finance preparation

If you can, put yourself in the position to make smart financial decisions. Decisions based on emotion are the greatest threat to smart financial decision-making. There are numerous aspects to finances when relationships end. Paul Clitheroe observed that he has:

> encountered a worrying number of women, in particular, who have handed the reigns of financial control entirely to their husband or partner only to have it cost them dearly, even when their marriage is very strong. And while it may seem to make life easier, it could see them struggling to convince a lender that they represent a low risk if they find themselves suddenly single at a later stage...Women tend to live longer than men, and many will find themselves managing their own finances at some point, even if it is years off into the future after their spouse has died.[23]

Women are especially vulnerable to financial disadvantage in their old age. This is more so for women who experience separation later in life. Factors contributing to this situation include low rates of participation in the paid labour force, disparities in pay equity between men and women, and the gender-specific burden of social/cultural labour required of women. These factors are compounded by the ageist discrimination in the paid workforce that affects women far earlier than men. Such discrimination diminishes paid work opportunities for women and escalates the odds of forced retirement and 'redundancy'. Older, single women are particularly vulnerable to poverty and isolation.

It is important that you learn as much as you can and ask questions if there are issues you do not understand. Consider some of the following financial issues.

Your 'financial identity'

If you are like others who have left the management of household financial affairs to your Ex, whether your relationship was heterosexual or same-sex, you will need to establish what is known as a 'financial identity'. As Paul Clitheroe says:

> Maintaining a savings account, and even a credit card of your own, lets you preserve your 'financial identity'. In other words, it gives you a documented record through your account statements of the way

> you save and handle credit. This will stand you in good stead ... [if] you need to apply for a loan or any type of credit in your name in the future.[24]

Use government benefits

If you are entitled to receive government benefits, be sure to apply for them. Contact your local agency. Check websites to find out what types of support payments may be available to you. Use search terms like welfare payments, income support, disability support, single parent allowance, and sickness benefits. In Australia, go to servicesaustralia.gov.au. In Canada, go to Canada.ca. In the UK go to gov.uk. In New Zealand go to newzealandnow.gov.nz. If you reside in America your state or county will have their own site. Financial assistance of various types will be available according to your circumstances. If you are a parent you may be entitled to some kind of family allowance benefit. You may also be entitled to free counselling sessions with a psychologist. It is more than likely that you will need to show recent tax returns.

Live within a budget

Going your separate ways means financial independence, especially if you and your Ex were together for a long time and built wealth. Financial independence requires having a disciplined approach to funding your lifestyle. The idea of a budget may seem uncomfortable, but it is necessary to achieve your financial base and balance for growing your future wealth. Whether or not you think your separation outcomes are unfair, you only need to read Paul Clitheroe's *Money, Marriage and Divorce* and Scott Pape's *Barefoot Investor* and *Barefoot Investor for Families* to know that your future can be financially positive and fulfilling.[25] Be sure to read books by Paul Clitheroe and Scott Pape to wise up on growing your own finances. Paul Clitheroe also has a magazine for everyone's personal finances, *Money*, and its website, moneymag.com.au Be sure to access this website, subscribe to the magazine, or regularly read it at your local library.

So, let's talk budgeting.

To budget you need to understand the bare basics of money. The level of financial literacy in Australia has been reported as alarmingly low. Paul Clitheroe, along with financial counsellors, would readily agree that creating a budget is easy. And yet many people fail to do so. In many circumstances this is because these people do not have this basic level of skill. The challenge is balancing your needs with your wants. Says the wise man Clitheroe:

> 'Needs' are very different from 'wants', and they include things like mortgage repayments or rent, utility costs, groceries, fuel and car loan repayments, and debt payments. These expenses must take top priority in your spending, because a whole range of unpleasant consequences will flow from not covering them – from having the electricity disconnected through to losing your home if you continually default on mortgage or rent repayments.
>
> There's almost always room to cut back on essential costs ... as long as (sic) you are committed to making the budget work. For instance, you may be able to save money on utilities by shopping around for a cheaper power provider. Refinancing your home loan could secure you a lower rate to reduce your monthly mortgage repayments. Something as simple as adding a few generic products to your supermarket trolley rather than opting for branded products can cut hundreds of dollars from your annual grocery bill. It may take a bit of effort to trim money spent on everyday essentials: the potential to pocket big savings makes the process worthwhile.'[26]

What can *you* take from Clitheroe's message? Do you budget at all? If you don't, it's time to get started. Keep your eye on the details. Do not lose sight of your goals.

Budgeting

Drafting a budget, however modest your resources, will be useful in steering you away from debt. Managing your money on your own can be overwhelming for many people. If you need the help of a financial counsellor, then seek one out. If you have a financially savvy and trustworthy friend, let them help you. Start by listing your current assets and liabilities as the broad features of your financial picture. List your wages/salary payments, income earned from business, family support payments (if relevant) and any returns on investments. These would include investments such as rental properties, shares, managed funds and term deposits. Be sure that you note after-tax amounts in your budget.

Essentially, the purpose of a household budget is to record money coming in against money going out. The everyday expenses will include electricity, telephone, rent, child support, after school care, loan repayments such as on a car, personal loans, credit cards and house repayments, fuel/public transport, groceries and clothing. You may think everyday items pale into insignificance against big ticket items like car registration, council rates and loan repayments, but you also need to keep the details of everyday items. Keep all receipts, no matter how small. Tracking your spending is essential to having a budget. You would be amazed how much those little 'treats' while shopping or that morning coffee or buying your work lunch instead of preparing it at home add up over a year. Keeping receipts will prove this to you. You need to decide on your budgeting priorities. You really do. And whatever you do, *avoid taking on debt.*

Financial records

Absolutely make sure that you make copies (for you and your lawyer) of all relevant financial records such as annual tax returns, bank account statements, salary records, superannuation statements, mortgage records, insurance records, lease records, loan or debt records, investment records, asset valuation records, and the like. If you have a small business, then you will need all relevant documents. If your former partner has a business and the financial documents of the business are accessible, then copy them. Copy the obvious, too, like all financial documents on your home computer. Your lawyer will be able to advise you on the records you need to take. Keep your record copies out of the house and in a safe place with a professional service, friend or family member. Many of these documents should be in your 'fearless folder'.

Review your sums

This task will be easy if you are an organised person who has kept records of your expenditures for the last three years. Organised people fare better in their separation because they have accurate financial records at hand. If you have not kept records, *start now*. Being organised and across the issues and information builds confidence and the feeling of being in control. Find a finance savvy, well-organised friend to help you, and consider making copies of your records to be kept secure by this person, or a trusted friend or family member. Set up a system for closely recording your expenses from the moment of separation—keep all receipts and methodically record your expenses. Create a ledger which details your monthly expenditures on utilities, household expenses, insurances, mortgage, etc. Determine how much you spend per day because this will help with planning your 'separation budget'.

Financially planning and budgeting to resource your decision to leave is essential. Get advice on issues like property settlement, spousal maintenance and child support. A financial advisor can advise you on superannuation and major asset issues and likely decisions required. Again, a reminder to make sure you arrange for one independent valuation expert to value the house you live in, whether owned jointly or not and share this cost with your Ex.

Earnings of your Ex

How much do you know about your Ex's finances? How much do they earn? Have you both had access to each other's earnings records, salary slips or pay stubs? Tax returns? If so, then take copies. If your Ex is self-employed and has other incoming cash flows, try to make sure you know what these amounts are. Business valuations can be tricky and complex. Try to find out as much as you can so that you can be across as many of the financial issues as possible. I understand that this can be a daunting prospect for people who are not finance savvy. Consider enlisting help from someone you trust who has finance skills.

Websites can help you with financial literacy and economic safety. For instance, women can access The Centre for Women's Economic Safety at cwes.org.au and womentalkmoney.org.au. Similar resources for men can be accessed at MensLine mensline.org.au. And all of you have a valuable resource in the Australian government's site moneysmart.gov.au and your local financial counsellor.

Some separating partners hide assets from the other. There are signs agreed upon by many financial advisors that your former partner may be hiding assets. Chapter six addresses this issue in greater detail.

Paid work

Your separation will impact on your paid work. Are you finding it tough to balance the changes you need to make at home with your work obligations? If so, be sure to discuss the situation with the right decision-maker at work so they can offer you the support you need. Make time to sit down with your manager, or if in a small business, your boss.

Whilst you might find it difficult to talk about your personal situation, this will help you deal with your work environment. You may not even be aware that your workplace can actually help you in your situation, and that your manager is obliged to provide you with support.

It is important that you know what kinds of support are available. Think about what you need. Time off for appointments? Flexible work hours for a couple of weeks until you sort out parenting arrangements? Access to a workplace support service? If you need to take a few days off to get yourself together, talk to your doctor and organise the necessary certificate to take some leave. If you know the kind of support you need, then be sure to raise this with your boss/manager. Your discussion should cover ways your workplace can support you until you get back on your feet.

If you have not undertaken paid work in quite a while, do you need to audit your work skills to determine if you need to refresh any skills or retrain to improve your employment opportunities? Have you conducted a realistic assessment of your earning potential if you have been out of the paid workforce whilst childrearing or being unemployed?

Joint accounts

Be sure to open a new bank account in your own name. Keep as little funds in any joint accounts as possible. Take action to prevent your Ex from transferring all of the money from your joint account, should you have one. Check any redraw facilities. Check whether caveats need to be placed on properties. Cancel your old credit card if you are the principal and arrange a new one.

Also, organising a credit card *before* separation will often be easier, especially for women who have maintained the home and cannot demonstrate ownership of individual financial resources or an income record.

Check any joint mortgage obligations and whether joint signatures are required. Make sure you close any joint credit cards if you are close to leaving. Check the status of joint superannuation/retirement accounts, any loans and take action as necessary. Check the legal ownership of your residential property and joint business. Make sure you redirect your wages to your *new* bank account. If you are in the fortunate situation to have a supportive family, then please take advantage of this—accept practical and financial help whenever it is available.

Insurance policies

Risk management matters no matter what stage of life you are in. Risk management is the reality of finance. And it is especially important following separation and divorce. You will need to amend your superannuation/ retirement fund and insurance policies to change the beneficiaries. Be sure that all of your amendments to these important documents accurately indicate your new circumstances and new priorities, place them in your 'fearless folder' and then store these documents somewhere safe. Be sure to check that your Ex has not attempted to cancel any policy which provides you with insurance cover (you may be surprised how many have attempted to do so!). Revise your life policies—total and permanent disability cover, trauma, critical illness cover, income protection cover, and health insurance.

Be sure to consider the adequate amount of cover in your new circumstances, including how to optimise tax deductibility.

Estate planning

For older people who have separated or divorced and are contemplating re-partnering, the issue of estate planning requires consideration in light of legal rules that apply. In many states/countries, including Australia, if you have made a will prior to remarriage then it is automatically revoked by remarriage, but *not* by separation or divorce. It is surprising how many people who re-partner neglect to change their will. Take the time to do a new will which documents your new intentions. If you have a Testamentary Trust, does this need to be changed? What other changes need to be made to named beneficiaries? Do the executors of your will need to change? Do not forget associated issues raised by your new will such as Power of Attorney arrangements and Advance Health Directives. Make a list of the changes you need to make to your estate planning. Be smart and attend to these issues as soon as you can.

Binding financial agreements for future relationships

Financial agreements are a must for older people who are contemplating re-partnering, especially when there are substantial assets to protect or limited remaining assets to further diminish. Such an agreement should set out arrangements for asset division should the relationship end. Agencies that record marriage statistics in Australia, UK, Canada, New Zealand, and America do not report promising statistics for second marriages since these have a higher collapse rate than first marriages. It would therefore be prudent for you to seriously consider the step of formalising a financial agreement, or pre-nup as it is called in some countries.

Divorce-proofing your retirement

It can be difficult for some people to plan properly for retirement. Few people are savvy enough to divorce-proof their retirement. By the time you take the step to become a 'silver separator', you will have almost completed the process of amassing assets and accumulated savings. Most people with the means to do so, focus on saving enough funds to ensure a financially comfortable retirement. Failure to divorce-proof your retirement means that you now only get to live on around half of that amount. Since both you and your Ex may have few years left to reap the benefits of paid work, there is little time to rebuild that wealth. This has serious repercussions for both parties, although your investment savvy can assist in lessening the financial risk involved in 'silver separation'.

Review your retirement vision

If you have always had a 'bucket list' or had great dreams to be fulfilled during your later years, your new financial situation may mean that it is time to do a reality-check and reprioritise your retirement goals. How will you fund these goals? Which goal is more important than others? Do you now have new goals? This is the time to recalibrate. You know that balancing your new financial situation with personal happiness will require careful thinking on your part. Diminished financial resources do not mean that personal happiness will be elusive. While maintaining the resolve not to allow emotional decisions to affect your financial decisions, smart financial decisions can serve to support personal happiness and peace of mind. Let's face it, financial decisions and personal happiness decisions require two different skillsets—and wisdom.

Fund your aged care

Across the world women make up the majority of caregivers (although research is needed regarding people of diverse backgrounds).[27] It is an uncomfortable thought, but one, regardless of gender, you may have to contemplate. What arrangements will you make for *your* care when you are no longer able to care for yourself? How will you go about putting money aside or managing your investments for this eventuality? Planning ahead will help give you peace of mind. Ensure that you make a detailed list of tasks to complete in order to fund your aged care.

Home sharing

There are a growing number or organisations in countries like Australia, Canada, United Kingdom, New Zealand and the United States which specialise in facilitating the matching of compatible individuals from all backgrounds to share accommodation. You need not wait until you are older to consider this financial opportunity to sustain your lifestyle. And you need not be battling the daily financial demands to take advantage of home sharing. However, it's possible that some of you may struggle with gathering sufficient resources to say, pay the upkeep on the home you have kept from your separation, and will have to face the option of sharing the expenses. You can explore home sharing opportunities on the internet. Depending on your own preferences for the kind of person you would like to share your home with, you can shape your options for the kind of expense-sharing, household duties, garden maintenance, social company, or other needs or wants you have. Obviously, your financial resources come first. That would be your starting point. This option is worth considering. You are never too old to begin something new!

Paying for your legal fees

The growing number of firms with finance options to help you pay your legal fees means that in countries like Australia, United Kingdom, Canada, New Zealand and United States, you cannot be 'held hostage' in your negotiations by your financial circumstances.

You have choices.

How you manage your choices can take the stress away, should you use your choices wisely. If money is tight you still have options which include legal aid, community legal services, and women's legal services. Typically these services require a donation. It is worth reading up on how these services can help you.

You may also decide to borrow money to pay for your legal fees. Think carefully about this decision. Borrowing money can have disastrous consequences. Many people borrow money from family and friends. Others may have the capacity to pay but choose to invest their money and borrow funds to cover their legal expenses. Others take out a loan from firms who have a standing arrangement with your family lawyer or the firm for which they work. Typically, this particular arrangement is possible only after you have retained a family lawyer and commenced proceedings. In this situation you will be required to give your lawyer consent to discuss your finances and separation situation with the finance lender who will then determine that it is safe for them to lend you the money that you will be required to repay. If you choose this option be sure to confirm with your lawyer that these lenders are qualified, accredited and registered with the government and relevant professional bodies in order to practice. You would also be wise to check the finance lender's record with the accreditation body.

This is called doing your 'due diligence'.

Both parties need to make sure that the loan is legitimate and repayable. It is a good idea to discuss this with your financial advisor or financial counsellor. Anecdotal information indicates that many women who do unpaid work in the home (e.g. 'stay-at-home-mums') find this option appealing. It means you cannot be bullied by your Ex by being told that you will be left 'with nothing' because you do not bring in an income.

Think about your options. You *will* be able to fight for a fair settlement and hire a good family lawyer.

Conclusion

Take all care to plan before you leave, if you can. If not, take the steps you need to leave safely. End your relationship as effectively as you can. You know only too well that sometimes you will not be able to plan as well as you would like. The dynamics of the relationship you want to leave could be volatile, with every day a new challenge. However, planning can make an important difference to not only ending the relationship, but *how* you end it. Use your organisational abilities and secure all the documentation you require.

And age *does* matter. There is every reason for you to enjoy your older years in a positive and refreshing fashion. There are many older separated individuals who have gone on to live wonderfully fulfilling lives, armed with a stronger attitude to life and a willingness to try new adventures. If you are in this age group, make sure you are up for new experiences to make the most of life!

Separation Preparation Checklist

- ☐ Safety
- ☐ Contact details
- ☐ Record your date of separation
- ☐ Let your support network know
- ☐ Inform your children's school/s
- ☐ Learn your legal rights and obligations
- ☐ Identify precious household items
- ☐ Complete household contents inventory
- ☐ Complete parenting considerations (see chapter 14)
- ☐ Draft parenting plan (see chapter 14)
- ☐ Create parenting diary (see chapter 14)
- ☐ Arrange financial resources
- ☐ Attend to paid work arrangements
- ☐ Bank account/credit card arrangements
- ☐ Review your sums
- ☐ Know the earnings of your Ex
- ☐ Be aware of signs of asset hiding (see chapter 6)
- ☐ Re-arrange insurance policies
- ☐ Re-arrange superannuation nominations, e.g. Do you have a Binding Death Nomination?
- ☐ Attend to specific 'Silver Separation' considerations

4
Decisions and dollars

Decisions can cost big dollars. Get it right and you save money. Get it wrong and you will take much longer to recover financially. This chapter aims to foster your ability to think financially rather than emotionally. Making poor emotion-based decisions will cost you more in legal fees. Once you understand the decision-making process, you can apply your separation decisions with greater skill. Sound judgements will save you money.

This chapter offers you opportunities to understand:

- the decision-making process
- how to increase your ability to make sound decisions
- the decision–consequence dynamic
- that anger undermines effective decision-making

Making decisions under stress

Decisions are designed to maximise gains and minimise losses.[28] Pressure can unduly influence both the small and large scale decisions you make. Part of this pressure is the enormity of the consequences of getting your decisions wrong. Separation decisions have important consequences, such as your future financial security, your relationships with your kids, your friendship networks, your job performance, and your health and wellbeing. These *will be affected*. Have no doubt that—this *will* be the case.

Nevertheless, people differ, as do separation situations. Avoid making decisions to end the anxiety of it all. Do your best to avoid procrastination.

Write down the short-term and long-term decisions required of you. This may help you manage your anxiety over the separation. These lists can demonstrate to you that decisions can be made in *small, achievable steps*. Besides, the very act of writing down your thoughts help you clear your thinking. Why not give it a go now and consider making a list of the decisions that you are reluctant to make? Are you aware of the consequences of each decision? If so, write them down.

What does 'decision-making' mean?

This book discusses decision-making in its basic forms—that of choosing between two or more actions. Separation and problem-solving decision-making go hand-in-hand. It requires you to choose between different solutions to a problem, dilemma or proposition. Decision scientists declare that decision-making is typically intuitive, reasoned or a combination of both.[29]

Intuitive decision-making derives from your past experiences and your personal values. This form of intuition (or 'gut feeling') is perception-based and *not* necessarily reality-based. Decisions based on your intuition are a product of a synthesis of your life experience and guiding values, and then applying them to an issue in question. As Roy E. Disney said, 'When your values are clear, making decisions becomes easier.' Does this resonate with you? Intuitive decision-making merits care and is best accompanied by what some refer to as a 'reality check'. *Why* do you have that 'gut feeling' and *why* is it more intense for certain issues than others? Can your intuition be substantiated? Sometimes your intuition is your best guide. Do not dismiss your intuition in your decision-making during your separation.

Reasoned decision-making, on the other hand, is decision-making based on evidence and expertise, such as facts and figures, legal and financial advice. When you deal with complex issues in your separation, arming yourself with the information you need to make decisions is a *must*.

Difficult or complex decisions are best made using *both* intuitive and reasoned decision-making. These two types of decision-making do not follow in order: intuition does *not* necessarily precede reasoned decision-making. Indeed, in the context of your separation and divorce, it can often be useful to assemble the information, facts, figures, legal and financial advice, and then ask yourself how you regard this knowledge. What *choices* does this material present you? Once you have made your preferred choice, how do you *feel* about this choice? Does it feel *right* for you?

Let's take a closer look at how you actually go about making decisions so that you can achieve your preferred outcomes and reshape your life.

Steps in the decision-making process

There are six key steps in the decision-making process. Let's explore these now. The aim here is to show you *how* you can make effective decisions.

1. Establishing an effective decision-making environment

Decisions need time. Time allows you purposeful reflection so that you can assess the issues at hand. This is the detailed labour of decision-making and planning. Consider setting aside a block of time each day to progress your decision-making. Managing the time you need to make good decisions and then scheduling them according to your deadlines requires discipline, especially when putting your head under a pillow or watching the tennis is far more appealing! You need time to make your lists, think through your future actions and their likely consequences.

You can apply this wisdom to your separation and the decisions required to protect your best interests. It's easy to get bogged down in the problem, make excuses, and/or get into the blame game. Getting stuck prevents you from developing solutions because you are focused on the problem and not the solution. Ask yourself, 'What is the outcome I am seeking?' , 'What do I want to achieve?', 'What do I want to happen?'. Work back from the outcomes to list the steps in answer to 'How can I get the results want?'.

This will compel you to focus on the *solution,* rather than the apparent unfairness of your situation. Remember, this is a *process* that you build on. Force yourself to move away from emotional thinking. This will allow you to generate new ideas. Focusing on the outcome keeps you in active problem-solving mode. Once you move into generating ideas then you can shift up a level to *generating* solutions and identifying consequences. Focusing on outcomes is the very best thing you can do because it immediately positions you firmly in the mindset of a problem-solver.

What is the vision of your life after separation? Stay faithful to this vision. The process I have just outlined will help you achieve that vision (provided it is reasonable and achievable).

Thus, an effective decision-making environment is one where you decide first of all to become *purposeful in your thinking* and in your *determination to progress your separation process.*

Perhaps you might even do this with a support team urging you on with positive encouragement (and not interference). At this point, identify your challenges by writing them down as a list of key questions. Step one: draw out some columns. Step two: in corresponding columns list your big questions and then your smaller questions. Step three: Match them with proposed solutions in the next column. This method will help you include your priorities and preferred outcomes.

Try this decision-making scenario. Write down all the questions you can think of and then try to prioritise them. Frame the big questions first. These might include:

- What are my choices?
- What are the possible outcomes? In the short-term? In the long-term?
- What are my priorities?
- How will my decisions affect those most important to me?
- What do I know about my Ex that will help me make the right decisions?
- What advice has my lawyer given me that resonates foremost in my decision-making?

- What are the types of information given to me by my lawyer that are more important than others?

You could even list your choices to address these priorities. The important thing is that you are fully aware of the consequences of the decisions you make before you act on them.

2. Generating potential solutions

Create a productive space in which to generate solutions. Develop as many practical alternatives as is reasonable. One type of knowledge worth storing is anecdotal knowledge; tips that are shared between those who have been through the challenges of separation. Of course, professional advice from your lawyer, financial advisor or other experts will be valuable in helping you make good decisions.

Deliberately choose a space in which to position yourself for calm reflection so that, cognitively, you can be receptive to solutions. How do you position yourself for calm reflection, you ask? Some suggest deep breathing exercises. Those of you familiar with meditation will identify the benefits of this exercise; or it may be other exercise in the form of what suits you best. Perhaps a stroll, swimming laps, or gardening.

These are all fuelled by the positive effects of exercise on your brain and body. Some even find the same benefits from thinking through things while having a long hot shower. Keep asking yourself questions to open doors in your brain that will devise solutions to the particular challenges you face. Some even pose questions before bed to 'sleep on it', as it were, since your brain still works while you are asleep. The ultimate point here is that you need to do what is right for *you* to create that productive space that will allow you to generate a solution.

3. Evaluating the solutions entails assessing risk, consequences and feasibility

Having framed your broad questions, identified your separation tasks, and generated some initial solutions, you are now positioned to head in the right direction for making decisions. How do you know if your decision is the right one? To evaluate your proposed solutions, which may become your decisions, you need to ask these questions:

- Will this decision produce the results I want? When? How?
- Is this decision cost-effective?
- Does this decision align with the professional advice I have been given?
- Do the rewards outweigh the risks?
- How does this decision impact on my financial resources?
- How will this decision impact on my well-being? My ability to cope?
- Is the best decision only for the short-term or does it serve the long-term more effectively?
- Is this decision positive for me as well as those I care about?
- Is this decision simply serving my short-term need to avoid conflict or please others?

It may help to keep a journal of the decisions you make and their rationale. Keeping a record of steps you have taken towards your decision-making may help you to audit the effectiveness of your decision-making and action planning. This is *your* journey. The underlying project management value of keeping a journal is that it will strengthen your decision-making capacity for your future, whatever the context. You may very well be surprised at the emerging benefits now *and* down the track that the process of separation offers you. It is, of course, up to you whether you take advantage of these.

4. Deciding what is right for you.

Deciding what will make a decision smart and 'right for you' sounds relatively unproblematic. How many times have you received unsolicited advice from family and friends eager to tell you what you should do? If only you 'did this or that then you'd be better off', they tend to say. It helps to keep such advice at bay by reminding yourself that this is not their separation but *yours*. Doing what is right for you is essential because separation situations vary. What may be right for your friend, sister, brother or neighbour may very well *not* be right for you. Audit your decision-making with fierce honesty.

Such fierce honesty needs to include your intentions and motivations for your communications with your former partner. You need to ask yourself the following questions:

Self-Audit Questions

Question	Yes/No
Am I being reasonable?	
Am I making emotional decisions rather than financial decisions?	
Am I succumbing to the cumulative effect of years of browbeating and abuse?	
Am I achieving progress by making smart compromises?	
Are my decisions driven by the desire to just get it all over with so I do not have any more stress and mess in my life?	
In my decisions, am I compromising my integrity?	
Am I making decisions I can actually live with?	
Do I truly understand the information given to me about the key decisions which will impact my future financial security?	
Do my decisions actively support the best interests of my children?	
Am I up to the task of *assertively* handling our separation to achieve a fair settlement or do I need help?	

Please take the time to respond to these self-audit questions. Consider your responses carefully. Doing so will fuel your clarity.

5. Checking the decision

Checking your decisions involves auditing any assumptions you have made. When doing this, it is important to remember that this separation decision-making step involves both intuitive *and* reasoned decision-making. Not all of your considerations will be objective, and this is okay. After you have completed this audit, it is a good idea to go through this assumption-checking with a trusted advisor who will give you feedback. You need to do what feels *right* for you in *your own situation*. What actions will logically bring you closer to achieving the outcomes you are seeking from your legal process?

Information has a hierarchy. Some information is more important and has consequences for your future. As such, it demands earlier action. Be sure to apply a reward/risk ratio when you audit your decision.

If you have made a decision that is not working out well for you, then *amend* your decision. Do not delay changing a decision that is not working. Own it and move on.

6. Communicating and implementing your decision

Communicating and implementing your decisions involves, first, ensuring that you can explain how and why you have reached the decision. Second, you need to be able to explain the soundness of your decision and its risk/reward ratio. Is this reasoning persuasive? For some people, devising a plan becomes an evolving process of small tasks that fit within a big picture of purposeful goals. This is fine, as long as it is productive and efficient. If the actual act of implementing your decisions is intimidating for you, or you are nervous about getting the ball rolling by taking practical steps in your separation, then perhaps you might benefit from the following:

- Arrange for someone like a trusted advisor to be with you when you take the actions you need to take.
- Say the things you need to.
- Rehearse what you want to say, perhaps with a trusted friend. Rehearsing builds confidence. Rehearsing can help people who are not adept at thinking on their feet.
- Practising what you want to say will help strengthen your composure. It will also help you control your breathing so that you can communicate calmly and clearly.
- Ensure that you attend to the obvious self-care actions—eat, sleep, hydrate—and get your schedule organised to start implementing your decision.
- Review the decision-making process you have taken yourself through. What are the results of your decision? Have you achieved the results you sought? Is it looking like success? What else do you need to do?

So, did you make the right decision? Or does it need to be amended?

There are other questions about which you need to be honest. Compliance with the wishes of your Ex can result in overcompensation, resistance, fear and intimidation. Complying with the wishes of your Ex can sabotage clear thinking about settlement issues. Ask yourself the following:

- How well do I know myself?
- How am I vulnerable to pressure from my Ex?
- Do I know what my demons are?
- Do I know under what conditions they surface?
- Do I know my triggers to self-destructive behaviours and self-destructive decision-making?

Self-awareness and self-honesty are crucial to being effective in your decision-making.

Smart decision makers have a Plan B. Having a back-up plan is smart because your separation progress obviously involves another party with interests that may be vastly different to yours. Build these likely differences into your planning and preparation. Arm yourself with knowledge. Knowledge is the best decision-making ally you can have!

Insight: Anger and decision-making

The fundamental rule of decision-making is to never make a decision while you are angry, in a panic, upset, sleep-deprived, hungry, under the influence of alcohol or other substances, grieving intensely or feeling overwhelmed by hurt, the desire for revenge or retribution, or other intense emotions. Psychological and emotional turmoil will sabotage clear thinking. It is amazing how many poor decisions have been made out of anger. Such turmoil undermines your ability to carefully think through issues, actions and consequences. Knowing when to hold off making a decision (and committing yourself to not making a decision) while you are emotionally charged will yield rewards and will certainly prevent regrets. Be smart about this.

The presence of pronounced anger during the separation process limits your legal options and drives poor decision-making. The brutal reality about anger is that it is ruinous to your separation. It will increase the cost of your legal fees, heighten the stress for both you and your Ex (as well as your lawyer), and delay finalising the legal aspects of your separation, all of which will impoverish your future lifestyle choices. It is a fact of life that not all people choose to separate the smart way. Many struggle with anger. I think it's worthwhile to take a closer look at anger and how it can be managed. It's important that the communication between you and your Ex remain constructive.

What is anger?

Professor Albert Ellis defines anger as 'a special combination of your thoughts, feelings, and behaviours, when you are (or think you are) severely frustrated by unfortunate conditions and by people's "unfair" behaviour'.[30]

More simply, psychologists view anger (as opposed to aggression) as a natural human emotion which can vary in degree and according to context.

In a reasonable context, modest anger and irritation can be managed constructively. There are likely to be situations in which either you or your Ex become 'hot under the collar', particularly when encountering different views and expectations. Both of you will continually face the reminder that not everything will go your way. Anger is a common way to express relationship conflict. Modest conflict should never be avoided in a relationship-separation context when there are important issues at stake. Conflict is merely a symptom of an emotion—it is a problem in play which has yet to be resolved.

Doing your separation the smart way is to recognise this fundamental reality. Recognise that each of you has the right to your own opinion. Recognising what your differences are and putting them on the table for discussion tackles the issue of conflict head on. If you are in a low conflict situation with your former partner, setting some ground rules about how you communicate when things start to get heated will help both of you. Boundaries are your allies in a difficult situation. They ensure that both you and your Ex treat each other with respect, even in disagreement. Such a commitment will open the way for mutually positive results.

Managing anger

Communicating constructively while being angry is hard. But it's not the only challenge you're facing in your separation process. As with taking the time to make smart decisions, take the time to explore your anger. Learn about it. Ask yourself what it's actually doing for you and put into practise the following suggestions.

Acknowledge that you are angry

Use 'I' statements to tell your former partner that you are angry and why you are angry. Do this without making accusations. Assure the other party that even though you are angry, you want to proceed with the discussion to resolve the issue at hand.

Take 'time out'

If you are in danger of behaving destructively, tell your Ex that you need 'time out' to calm down. Reassure your former partner that you are not using 'time out' to avoid the issue, but to calm down so that you can resolve the issue in question. Make sure you suggest that you both make a time in the near future to continue the discussion. Close the conversation respectfully. If you do not, then you will very likely invite resentment and a lack of cooperation.

Reflect

Reflect on why you became angry during the discussion. Get to the *real* issues. Was it more than simply not having your wants met? What was the trigger? What do you consider might be the underlying cause of your anger? If your reflections are fruitful and your former partner is open to a brief explanation for your anger when you next talk, then why not share your thoughts? It is likely your Ex will feel respected, provided that you take responsibility for your behaviour and feelings. Do not shy away from apologising for calling a halt to the discussion. Apologies are highly underrated. 'I'm sorry' are two very powerful words which no one should avoid saying. Apologising does not mean that you are accepting blame for every negative behaviour in the former relationship. It simply means that right now you take responsibility for the behaviours you expressed that may have been difficult for your Ex.

Compromise is not weakness

When your wants are not met or your preferred arrangement is unacceptable to the other party, try to find out if there is a middle ground that can be reached. Is there an arrangement that both parties can live with? The ability to compromise and understand that flexible problem-solving is a strength can, if practised regularly during the separation negotiation, make your life easier. Remember—and repeat it to yourself as often as you need to—*Don't always be right. Be realistic.*

Pick your battles

You will know what your priorities are. Persuading your Ex that the arrangement you are seeking is fair to both of you, is a task best done with clear thinking and calm, steady resolve. Expressing anger if you encounter reluctance will only ensure that you will *not succeed*. There is give and take, middle ground, compromise and all the other negotiation and conflict-resolution terms to be used in persuasion. Remember, your Ex is more likely to respond cooperatively if you have demonstrated *your* ability to compromise. Put yourself in their shoes. Would you cooperate with someone who prefers to treat you disrespectfully, selfishly and angrily? If you care about fairness, then pick your battles.

Listen actively

Make it very apparent in the discussion that you are listening actively to your former partner's views. Is it too much to ask that you be flexible in your consideration of options for resolving the issue? Be sure to convey your commitment to working together to achieve a solution that is fair to both parties. Take their words into account and make it clear that you acknowledge them, even if you don't necessarily agree with them. How many times have you uttered the phrase, 'if only they would just listen?' Well, that is a two-way street.

Agree to disagree

There are some issues which will not be agreed on. Life is like that. This is where you, in a non-threatening way, suggest to your former partner that a mediator or arbitrator might help since this issue seems to be too difficult for you both to resolve on your own. Ask yourself, 'How important is the issue?' During these conversations, focus on the priorities—on what really matters. Being focused and staying focused will help you stave off any itchy inclinations towards impatience and anger.

Stay in the now

If accumulated resentments are impairing your ability to see the issues for what they really are, and undermining your ability to listen carefully to the other party's perspective *then cease fire!* You can only come to workable agreements with your former partner if you deal with the here and now, the issues which merit your undivided attention *now*. How genuine is your commitment to resolving as many issues as possible and getting on with your life? Know that you need to let go of the stings and bruises. The blame game is for dummies. Deal with the present. The future you want will come sooner.

Try to be understanding

If your former partner messes up in these sensitive discussions, then be prepared to extend some understanding rather than resorting to anger and shooting your mouth off. Acknowledge that a number of the discussions you have will be sensitive, uncomfortable and/or difficult. Remind them that you are committed to hanging in there to achieve solutions that each of you can live with. This too will firm up your conviction on days when your own commitment is on shaky ground.

Know who you are

Having a set of core values that you hold dear will steer you through this tough time. If someone close to you behaves badly, that is not an excuse for you to do the same. Walk away from anger, especially when it's yours.

Get real and stay real

Nothing about separation is easy and pain-free. These new arrangements in your life will not be perfect or exactly as you want them. They will be what is fair to *two* people, not one. There were two people in your previous relationship. Start these discussions with your Ex by being realistic.

Seeking help

There is no shame in asking for help to manage your anger. None. At the end of this chapter, you will find a basic list of sources to access anger management assistance. The list is brief, largely because there are few government agencies that provide specific anger management programs. Many of the providers are in private practices. Such programs are often subsumed within more general programs. For instance, they may form one section of a course or part of a series of psychological treatment. You are best advised to discuss matters with your doctor, who can refer you to a reputable source of assistance.

Seeking help is a smart move. It means that you recognise that your anger is a problem for you and is damaging relationships with those close to you. You realise that people close to you get hurt by your anger. And maybe they get hurt repeatedly. You are brave enough and smart enough to say to yourself, 'Hey, I've done it again. This is getting out of hand. I have to change my life, and I have to do it before I lose everyone who matters to me'.

If you choose to go to a psychologist who specialises in anger management, your first consultation might look something like this.

Psychologist: *Hi ______ How can I help you today?*

You: *Well, (pausing) I seem to be getting angry and it seems to get the better of me.*

Psychologist: *Hmm (thoughtfully understanding without judgement). That's not good. How long has this been happening?*

You: *It seems to be getting worse and worse. My partner's left me and I'm basically stuffed.*

Psychologist: *When you say you get angry, can you describe for me what you mean? And how often does this happen?*

You: *My Ex walked out when I yelled at her/him for the hundredth time. Anything just sets me off and I hate it. I hate me. I've ruined everything.*

Psychologist: *Right. It seems we have some things to talk about. Are you prepared to work on managing your anger? This will not happen overnight. It may take several sessions.*

You: *Yes. I have to.*

Seeing a psychologist is not a mark of shame. If managing your anger can improve your quality of life, isn't it worth the undertaking? Isn't it one of the best decisions you can make? For further discussion of consulting a psychologist, see chapter twenty-one. Remember, hot collars cost dollars. Seeking help to manage anger can not only save you money in the long run (by minimising a protracted separation), but it can improve relationships with those who matter to you.

Conclusion

Decision-making is a skill that can be learned. And it can be improved with practice. In reality, your separation often means that you *quickly* get plenty of practice at making decisions and implementing them. The more you make decisions and implement them, the stronger your confidence and self-esteem will become. And that is not such a bad thing, is it?

Sources of Anger Management Support

Organisation	**Contact Number**	**Website**
Australia		
Lifeline Telephone Crisis Support (includes multilingual support)	13 11 14	lifeline.org.au
Men's Adapt Change Programs	6468 303 707	adaptprograms.com.au
Blokes Psychology	(03) 9994 1721)	blokespsychology.com.au
Head to Health	see website	headtohealth.gov.au
Managing Anger MensLine Australia	1300 78 99 78	mensline.org.au
SEA Change Anger Management for Women	1300 543 396	relationshipmatters.org.au

Organisation	Contact Number	Website
PLAG (parents and friends of lesbians and gays — Australia & Worldwide	see individual branches	pflagaustralia.org.au plfag.org (for other countries)
New Zealand		
The Complete Guide to Anger Management Courses in Auckland	see website	therapycounselling.net/narrative-counselling-nz
Effective Anger Management for Women	see website	studyspy.ac.nz
United Kingdom		
The British Association of Anger Management	see website	angermanagerment.co.uk

SECTION 2
DISCLOSURE

5
Records, documents and filing

The purpose of this chapter is to discuss separation-relevant documents and their organisation in order to foster the efficiency of your paperwork management. Being organised will help you maintain control of the information flow, maintain clear thinking and feel in control of your role in the separation process. Having the information your lawyer needs ready and organised can help you save a considerable amount of money on legal fees. Making it easy for your lawyer to help you = dollars saved.

This chapter offers you opportunities to understand:

- how the effective organisation of information can save you money on legal fees
- different ways of organising your information
- the information you will need to give to your lawyer

What documents tell you

The resources you accumulate during your relationship, and those *you* bring to the relationship, are represented in documents. These documents are essential to enable your family lawyer to assess and advocate for your fair share of those resources.

What is a fair settlement? What is required for maintenance and child support? In order to represent you, your lawyer needs to have hard copies or electronic copies (maybe both) of these documents made available.

Here's where you can save yourself some money.

It is in your interest to have hard copies of your documents *at the ready* because legal fees for photocopying the originals of numerous documents can be quite high. Doing your own photocopying is a legal expense you can save yourself.

At your first meeting with your lawyer, make sure you tell them that you will—or have already completed—the photocopying and electronic copying of the documents required. Many people have shared tales of nasty surprises at being charged AU$1.00 or more per sheet for photocopying. Such nasty surprises only fuel distrust of lawyers' business practices. If the matter is complex, your lawyer may express a preference for having the firm manage all document reproduction. You may decide to ask why this is the case. This decision is up to you.

If, for any reason, you do not have possession of some of the documents you need, then consider taking copies of what you do have and dropping them off or posting them to your lawyer. If your access to needed documents is time-sensitive (for example, if your 'intended Ex' is out of the house and you want to copy them and return them as soon as possible), then grab what documents you can, copy them, and get them to your lawyer. If you are not sure whether they are relevant, copy or photograph them anyway.

Which documents do you need?

Do not delay until you have the perfect organisation of your documents. Get whatever copies you can to your lawyer, whenever you can. And remember, full disclosure is required. Hiding documents will not be viewed favourably by the Court. Failing to provide full disclosure can carry a serious penalty (this is discussed in the next chapter).

Organising the records of your separation requires a system of record-keeping. A filing system organised chronologically or by category/topic stored safely will be valuable in helping you retrieve records easily, prevent delay, and reinforce your grasp of document content and purpose. When you have a filing system in place, you will be able to easily access information for your lawyer, make decisions with the relevant facts in front of you, and maintain continuing awareness of all of the issues you need to be across in order to finalise your settlement.

Below you will find a list of documents your lawyer will require, depending on your circumstances. People's financial profiles differ, so circle the records that are relevant to you and start getting them together in a file. Be sure to clearly identify the file as follows:

- bank statements
- credit card statements
- tax returns
- real estate deeds
- income statements
- pay slips
- superannuation/retirement funds
- employment benefits
- employment contracts
- stocks and other options
- trust agreements
- investment records such as brokerage statements
- loan applications
- debts
- insurance records
- wills and power of attorney
- medical records
- inventory of household possessions

Where access to children is contested and parenting conflict is present, you might like to consider the following documents. Remember, any records or documents that demonstrate *your care-giving, stability and continuity* may be relevant, such as:

- family calendars
- report cards
- photographs
- appointment diary
- examples of schoolwork
- drawings
- sporting and recreational activity records
- children's cards and notes to you

In the case of high conflict or abuse the following documents will assist:

- texts
- emails
- phone messages
- hospital records
- police reports
- photographs of injuries

Record and document your activities as primary carer

Document your own contact with your children. Reflect on the tasks you perform. List them. Try to be as detailed as you can. If you are a primary carer, this list will no doubt be extensive. It will include describing the contact you have with your children and listing the parenting tasks you perform. Time-consuming? Yes. But it is worth doing. For instance, if you keep a weekly schedule posted on the refrigerator which identifies the activities relating to your children, then keep copies of each week's schedule. If your children bring home artwork for you to put on display, be sure to keep copies *and date them.* Keep records of your children's health, sporting, music, recreational and social activities.

If your children are older and in their teens, then conduct your record-keeping in a similar fashion. If this seems excessive, remember that the division of assets may be more straightforward than parenting arrangements. Parenting—that is, effective, responsible parenting—is the hardest job in the world. And when you have another parent in the picture who may have different priorities for the children and who might have different ideas about parenting, there will always be the potential for conflict. This can be the case even *after* a Parenting Agreement (discussed in detail in chapter thirteen) has been approved by both parents. Once agreements have been signed off, think of your record-keeping as a preventative measure and thorough administration of good parenting.

If your children spend time with significant others, such as your parents and/or the parents of your former partner, take the time to reflect on these relationships and the communications and activities involved, and document them accordingly.

Keep a 'child file' on what you observe about the other parent's contact with your children. Note the following:

- Do they keep appointments?
- Where do they go to spend time together?
- What time do they spent together?
- What gifts do they give the children?
- How is their communication style?
- What food is eaten by the children?
- How are the children's demeanour after spending time with the other parent?
- Does the other parent return the children late?
- Does the other parent meet their parenting obligations?

It's up to you to reflect on your own individual situation and record details you think are necessary. However, it should be noted that in circumstances of doubt, the more information you record, the more complete a picture you can provide for your lawyer to be used in assisted negotiation.

Be reasonable about this.

You are not conducting a witch hunt, you are recording relevant observations regarding your children and the other parent. Remember why you are recording this information in a specially organised 'child file'—to protect the best interests and wellbeing of your children.

Conclusion

Being familiar with the contents of your documents and their organisation will empower you to identify any inaccurate claims made by the other party.

Any and all records relating to your contact with your children are relevant. So, too, is documenting contact between your children and the other parent. Keeping records about your children is not only relevant to potential conflict about contact with your children, but such records will assist the Court in determining what is in your children's best interests.

Being organised and ensuring that you present your lawyer a complete picture of your circumstances will save you money on billable hours, copying costs, and energy.

6
Deceit, lies, and separation

The purpose of this chapter is to address the possibility of deceit in the legal aspects of your separation process. During separation, deceit, and your failure to detect it, can result in great expense for you. Deceit can emerge in many forms. It can deprive you of resources you will need for your future. If you know for sure that your Ex has been dishonest during your past relationship, being alert to deceit will assist your separation preparation as well as your management of the separation process.

This chapter offers you opportunities to understand:

- the seriousness of deceit in the family law process
- the types of deceit in the family law process
- clues to spotting asset hiding, lies and other types of deceit

Lying in family law matters

Many people tell lies during family law matters. Such people tend to tell lies 1) because of shame or embarrassment; 2) because of pure greed and revenge; and/or 3) to secure custody of children. Sometimes they tell lies which involve all three motivations.[31] How and why people tell lies during family law matters is highly revealing about who they are, and about the family law process.

If you were to tell lies during Court proceedings, this would be called 'perjury' and is a criminal offence. There are typically two ways people can tell lies during Court proceedings. The first is when people submit untruthful content in their written statement confirmed by oath or affirmation to be used in evidence in Court (known as an affidavit). The second is when people are giving evidence in the witness box.

Emotions belong to the side. Progressing tasks belong front and centre. And starting your separation-free future should be firmly fixed as your goal. For instance, by the time you get to Court any misdeeds committed by either party will very likely have been exposed: violence, infidelities, abuse of children, and/or a variety of unreasonable behaviours. Few people under pressure of conflict and unhappiness look good.

Be realistic in your expectations of what your lawyer can uncover. Some things are difficult to prove. Herein lies one of the three greatest temptations to deceive. Don't do it. You can be penalised. It will certainly cost you your credibility, whether or not you deserved it in the first place.

Judges are only too familiar with the experiences endured by separating couples. Judges work with the relevant legislation and deal with the facts that are relevant to the matter before them. It doesn't matter to them whether you are a nice person, a highly moral person or a flawed person. Judges do not care who left whom and why.

Their job is to manage the dispute according to the law.

The situation is what it is. Do not tell lies, attempt to disguise or mitigate any facts. Judges have seen it all. Should you decide to be loose with the truth, doing so cannot only be financially expensive, you can inflict long-lasting hurt on those who matter most to you. While many people have found the Court system excruciatingly slow, frustrating and outside their control, never mess with the judge. Judges are not silly. They do not appreciate untruthful conduct and can use the provisions in the relevant legislation to penalise you for doing so.

False allegations

Making false allegations of violence and/or abuse is one of the three typical ways people tell lies during family law matters. It is actually often a mix of the second and third reasons, which is revenge and child custody. You are probably familiar with scenarios in which parents try to influence children against the other parent. No matter how you regard the other parent (and they may well deserve your disdain), it is not appropriate to express your views regarding the other parent in front of your children. It most certainly breaches a principle that the Court upholds uncompromisingly: the principle of 'the best interests of the child' (discussed in chapter fourteen). Such public fractious conduct only hurts your children.

Should the Court find that you have been attempting to influence your children against the other parent, the Court is in a position to order you and the other parent to refrain from negatively commenting about the other parent to your children.

Where things escalate to criminal conduct is if one parent makes false allegations against the other parent. There have been numerous cases reported in which serious psychological damage to the children occurs because one parent makes false allegations against the other parent in order to gain custody of the children. Allegations have often included abuse, especially sexual abuse.

Long-term damage to relationships between parents and children, damage to the health of children, and legal penalties are to be expected in such circumstances. All of this leads to delay and expense. Don't do it.

Financial disclosure

Earlier, I discussed the reasons for lying in family law processes such as shame, humiliation and child custody issues. Now we come to greed. It is an offence to hide financial assets. You and your Ex are obliged to provide complete and thorough 'financial disclosure'. Pure greed and heightened resentment are key motivations for people to tell lies and be unwilling to fairly divide the asset pool. The experience of family lawyers is that it is often men who feel a sense of entitlement to keep their superannuation and most of the assets as they perceive themselves as having earned them. If children are involved, depriving the other parent of resources to care for your children is simply unsavoury. And your children will not forget that you have done this.

You risk significant penalties if you are discovered to be in breach of full financial disclosure. Deceit of this kind is considered to be a grave disrespect to the Court, not to mention that you are in breach of the legislation. The risk of penalty is not worth it. Failure to provide full and frank financial disclosure may include failing to list property held overseas, such as real estate, investments, bank accounts and antiques. For further detail see the discussion on asset hiding later in this chapter.

If you and your Ex have opted for a Binding Financial Agreement (outside of Australia, it's referred to as a Prenuptial Agreement), the Court can intervene in many states/countries, if a failure by you or your Ex to deliver full and frank disclosure is discovered. And what's more, the Court has no time limit on this authority. If you or your Ex have failed to disclose assets and it's discovered years later, you or your Ex can apply to have the Orders overturned. Again, it will be expensive for the offending party.

Is your lawyer finance savvy?

Deceit can cost you money. One of the first emotions ignited at negotiating the division of property is suspicion. You feel that you need to be alert to everything you are told. But here's the thing. While you might be worrying about your Ex being dishonest, do not be distracted by this. Be sure to get a sense of how savvy your *lawyer* is to spotting deception. This is not an offensive comment about your lawyer. This is project management. This is you making sure that your purchase of legal services is money well spent.

You want your lawyer to be:

- financially savvy, especially when it comes to your property settlement and the consequences of your decisions regarding property settlement[32]
- conscientious in their review of your documentation and the documentation provided by your Ex to spot omissions and inaccuracies
- alert to the signs of possible asset hiding by your Ex
- alert to possible deception by your Ex
- assert themselves appropriately in discussions of finance
- aware of the working reputation of the lawyer representing your Ex
- astute in their response to possible claims of your abusive conduct
- be alert to signs of financial abuse
- be sensitive to over or under valuations.

A note on financial abuse

Throughout this book I've gone to some length to show you the serious repercussions of leaving all the financial management matters to your Ex. Are you one of these people? While this is worrying, what is more concerning is the alarmingly high proportion of people who are financially illiterate. When it comes to money matters such as budgeting, understanding the value of goods, understanding the importance of saving, and understanding banking and how it works, a large proportion of people succumb to feeling overwhelmed. Many people are simply not confident when it comes to dealing with money. This leaves them vulnerable to financial abuse. Professor of Economics, Ross Guest, defines financial literacy as 'the ability to make sound financial decisions based on knowledge, skills and attitudes, taking into account personal circumstances.'[33]

Examples of financial abuse are depriving another of financial independence and control, wilfully taking over the financial management of the household and investments, giving the other partner pocket money, expecting the abused partner to account for every cent spent, and placing the other person in debt without their knowledge or consent.

Financial abuse happens across all social groupings in society. Family lawyers should be well-placed to recognise this because of the necessity for financial disclosures in family law matters. This is especially the case when financial disputes are acute and the financial abuse, particularly in complex financial matters, are ongoing, even after the relationship has been dissolved.

Are *you* being financially abused? It is important that you learn and understand the expressions of financial abuse. During many separations, one partner often comes to the realisation that this is one of the most incapacitating aspects of the domestic abuse they have endured. This reality is brought into the limelight particularly during relationship separations of older people. Make sure you tell your lawyer if you have concerns.

Asset Hiding

Dishonesty, in the form of asset hiding, merits your attention so that you can be alert to the signs should this issue present itself in your separation situation. Be sure to inform your lawyer if you think it likely that your Ex is hiding assets, so it can be detected, proven and rectified. Not taking any action at all could prove very expensive and have serious consequences for your financial future.

Hiding assets is made much easier if one of the partners is not involved in the management of household and financial matters, including investments. Being uninformed and uninvolved in the family finances is a recipe for disaster. It is mostly men in heterosexual relationships who typically control the family finances, and who tend to hide assets either in preparation for separation or during the process itself. They do so by overstating debts, reporting lower revenue than usual, reporting higher expenses than usual, and hiding, transferring, understating, and/or undervaluing particular assets.

Think carefully about the financial matters in your household. Perhaps grab a piece of paper and assess your level of financial literacy. Consider the following questions:

Assess your financial literacy

- Do you consider yourself to be a person who is knowledgeable about financial issues, or are you partially informed or confused by financial issues?
- Do you engage in household budgeting?
- Regardless of the nature of your relationship, reflect on how involved you were in the financial side of things compared to your Ex.
- Did you try to avoid financial issues and happily let your Ex take responsibility for the management of your finances and decision-making, such as budgeting, debt and investment management?
- Which financial issues do you struggle with now that you are separated?

When separation is at your door, it is too late to tell yourself that you should have been proactive in handling the family finances. To counter this issue, you must know where all of the key documents are stored, and you are able to photocopy, scan, or photograph those documents. And if you cannot locate your financial records, find out why. What reasons could there be for financial records being kept from you? A common reason is asset hiding.

It does not matter how well educated or how intelligent you are. Your spouse can be hiding assets from you when separation is on the horizon. Do you know the signs of asset hiding? Would you be able to tell if assets were being hidden?

The reality is, there are numerous ways your Ex can hide your assets from you during your relationship and in your settlement proceedings. Hiding funds in offshore bank accounts is a tried and true method which is difficult to uncover. Hiding behind the 'corporate veil' is another method which has been effective.

Hiding assets, income and/or debt is a breach of family law in many countries. It can attract a formidable penalty if this deception is detected during the legal process of property settlement. Each party has to be willing to report the non-disclosure and asset hiding to bring accountability and justice to their property settlement. And you need to be able to afford the expense of forensic accountancy services. Ironically, it is principally women who are disinclined to report deceit. They make this decision because they want the separation finalised. They want the stress and conflict to be over with. Is this you? Understanding the signs of deceit will help you become more proactive.

What to look for

Here are some red flags financial advisors share with their clients about asset hiding. I encourage you to reflect on these, whether you have already begun your separation process or are seriously considering separating from your partner.

Red Flags of Asset Hiding

Change in storage	Any change in the handling of finances is a red flag. If your financial statements, bank statements and other financial documents have typically been delivered to your home address and they no longer are, then be alert. Why has this changed? Why do you no longer have ready access to these documents? Telephone your bank and credit companies to check that assets or income are not being diverted. Ask for your own copies. Find out the address to which the financial records are being mailed/emailed.
Mishap	If your spouse has been the one in control of the finances and suddenly has a 'mishap' with the computer crashing, the hard drive disappearing or appearing 'damaged' and losing all of your financial data, then this is cause for careful review of what is actually going on.
Travel	If your spouse travels to countries with relaxed banking and taxation laws, do you know why?

Furtive conduct	If your spouse is now acting secretively about financial matters and is aggressive, defensive, controlling or simply dismissive when you ask about financial issues, this should alert you to the possibility of asset diversion or dissipation. To confirm your suspicion, consider hiring a forensic accountant.
Addiction	If it is apparent that your spouse has an addiction to illicit substances, prescription drugs or alcohol, or an intensifying gambling habit, financial abuse and escalating debt typically accompany this type of conduct.
Check listed loans, payments, and asset transfer	Financial advisors know all of the tricks people have pulled, including listing fabricated loans to relatives (who will repay after the settlement has been completed) and overpayments to the tax office, knowing that reimbursement will follow at a later date.
Change in income	If there is a change in your spouse's income circumstances, find out why. Are they suspending commissions until after the separation or divorce settlement has been finalised? Are they deferring a salary portion to some point in the future? Have they redistributed salary deductions to accommodate future intentions?
Cooking the books	If your spouse's business suddenly experiences Sudden Income Deficit Syndrome then something is up. There are numerous ways financial records can be 'amended'. Your forensic accountant and business valuation expert will be useful here. The lower the valuation of the business, the lower your settlement will be. You need to be protecting your financial security, so be bold. The relationship is over, so do not worry about causing offence by insisting on a forensic audit.
New bank account	If you discover (and do ensure that you are resourceful enough to do so or enlist the right expertise) that your Ex has established one or more new business and/or personal bank accounts and has not declared it, then this should alert you to the possibility that this account is being used to divert income and other funds in secret.

Suspicious? Tell your lawyer. This is why reflecting on the honesty and dishonesty of your Ex is important. Remember to write down the dishonest activities you recall from your relationship. Remember that asset hiding can involve other behaviours, so be wary of any type of furtive conduct during your relationship and separation proceedings.

Sexually transmitted debt

There is another type of financial deceit about which you need to be wary. Regardless of the type of relationship you have, 'sexually transmitted debt' can leave people nursing serious emotional and financial wounds.[34]

> 'Sexually transmitted debt', or 'relationship debt', is a serious problem. It happens when one person becomes liable to pay the debts or other financial obligations of their spouse or partner' ... Co-signing a home loan or having a joint credit card with your spouse can make you responsible for your other half's debt. Sexually transmitted debt goes a step further: the victims are often unaware they could become responsible for a spouse or partner's debts.
>
> A common scenario is being asked by your partner to act as a guarantor for a personal loan taken out in their name, or for a commercial loan for their business. It's a request that may be made lightly, with suggestions that your signature is a mere formality, or it may be accompanied by a great deal of pressure. In some cases, people agree to act as guarantor to keep the peace.
>
> In fact, agreeing to be a guarantor is a serious business. You won't get any rights to the asset financed by the loan, but you become responsible for repaying the loan if the original borrower...cannot or won't meet the repayments. This can put you in a position of having to sell personal assets, including your home, to pay off the debt. Alarmingly, research has shown that in the past, around two-thirds of people named as guarantors on loans were women.[35]

Insight: Lies, deceit and clues

I hope to foster your understanding of the ways and means of deceit in a bid to strengthen your ability to spot deception. The mission of this chapter has a flip side. Be discerning in your suspicions. If you go running down every rabbit hole of suspicion you will be spending a lot of money. Do not do this. Not all dishonesty can be proven. Your instincts may tell you something is going on, your familiarity with the flawed behaviour of your Ex may alert you to something out of the ordinary, but if you cannot meet the legal threshold of proof then you will waste your money, time and energy. Be smart. Get through your legal process sooner, spend less than you might, and come out the other side with as many resources as you can. Be savvy, but do not spend money that you do not need to.

But let's look at deception in general. In his pathbreaking book *Telling Lies,* pioneer researcher Professor Paul Ekman defines a lie 'as a deliberate choice to mislead a target without giving any notification of the intent to do so. There are two major forms of lying: concealment, leaving out true information; and falsification, or presenting false information as if it were true'.[36]

Deception experts generally concede that fibs, white lies, politeness and tact, exaggeration or boasting are very much different to what are referred to as 'serious lies'. And some 'serious lies' are more serious than others. Some are malevolent. Deceit during family law matters is very serious and can have critical consequences. 'Serious lies' are at the other end of the continuum of lying—they do not approximate the social lies people tell to grease the wheel of politeness. Have you ever told any 'serious lies'? How would you describe *your* level of honesty? How would you describe the level of honesty of your former partner?

Apparently, on average, an individual tells two major lies per day. One third of all normal conversations includes some element of lying (this figure rises to 80% when it comes to job applications). Even more alarmingly, four out of every five lies go undetected.[37] Can you tell when you are being lied to? Do *you* lie? What about? Is there a pattern to your lying? Now look at this issue from another perspective. What impacts have being lied to had on you? How did you discover you were being lied to?

Why can't we tell when someone is lying?

Did you know that most people cannot tell when someone is lying to them? Why? The most significant reason relates to what researchers call 'excessive credulity'. You typically start off by trusting other people and believe they are telling the truth, until there is evidence to the contrary. What's more, even when you become aware that lying exists in the interaction, you greatly overestimate your capacity to distinguish between lies and the truth.[38] Many a credible scientific experiment has been conducted, the results of which prove that only half of the general population can spot deceit half the time, whatever their age, sex or occupation. And you would think that police, judges, lawyers and psychiatrists perform much better than the general population. Research validates that they, too, overestimate their capacity to tell between truth and lies (but are better than most).[39]

What's more, your ability to tell truth from lies is far worse when you know the other person well. The better you know someone, the less capable you are of detecting their lies. Strangers are better at detecting lies than acquaintances.[40] So someone you know, like your Ex, can get away with lying to you more easily than not.

When you think about your ability to tell if someone is lying to you, you have certain assumptions at play or rely on stereotypes. For instance, you may assume liars betray themselves by looking shifty and evasive, wringing their hands, and fidgeting and shifting in their seats. The opposite is what frequently occurs. Liars almost always take care to look the person they are dealing with straight in the eye, ensure that their body language matches their words, and adopt a posture expressing conviction and sincerity.[41] It's easy to be misled by looks and gestures over which the liar exerts great control. The face reveals more deceit than words used by the liar. People should be more attentive to the voice and body than they are. It is difficult to separate voice and emotion. Deceit can be revealed by the sound of the voice including shifting to a different pitch.

A liar tends to reveal fewer details than a person who is telling the truth. For example, they use fewer words. Discomfort at being questioned leads liars to think too much about their replies. They choose their words carefully and sometimes curtail debate by saying they need to discuss the matter at a later time or show relief at an interruption. Liars' guilty feelings encourage them to talk less about themselves and to use the word 'I' less. This is called 'psychological distancing'. In contrast, a liar has more of a tendency to spontaneously cite the importance of 'ethics' or the value of 'intellectual honesty' and to call for trust. 'Trust me.' 'Believe me.' 'Frankly, I am telling you the honest truth.' Honest people rarely talk about ethics in such contexts.[42]

It is worth reading Paul Ekman's book, *Telling Lies,* if you want to learn more about deception, since I have touched only on a few crucial points. If you suspect that your Ex is lying about key issues, challenge them by revealing your scepticism and asking numerous questions. In particular, apply the wisdom of Professor Maurice E. Schweitzer, an American lie detection specialist.[43] Ask your Ex different questions on the same subject, asking for details that you would expect your Ex to know and others your Ex would not know, raising issues out of chronological order, and posing apparently simple questions for which your Ex will not necessarily be prepared. By doing this, it is possible that deceit by your Ex will be revealed. This may be done with your Ex making inconsistent claims or, more simply, struggling to articulate a response to questions that should require no effort. By posing an array of specific questions from the outset, you also reduce the probability of having to deal with lies. Lies will cost you money to unearth and prove.

Conclusion

Be alert to complying with the requirements of honesty in the family law process. Do this or unwanted complications will arise. Should the issue of dishonesty from your Ex arise in the form of lying during the legal process or failing to disclose assets, then take action. Do not let suspicion distract you from progress. Whatever you do, keep moving forward to the completion of your separation.

SECTION 3
SMART COMMUNICATION

7

How to suggest the way forward to your Ex

The purpose of this section is to provide you with an overview of the strategic communication skills upon which you can draw, depending on the option you select for your legal process. When you reach section four of this book, you will see that each legal pathway demands the use of particular communication skills. Sensitivity, clarity, and transparency are important in communication with your Ex, should your circumstances allow negotiation and cooperation. Your initial decisions will likely be based on whether your separation is high or low conflict. High conflict will limit your options. This chapter will help you stay in control of your legal process if you are in a relatively low conflict separation. You can do this by persuading your Ex of the most constructive legal pathway for dissolving your relationship.

This chapter offers you the opportunity to understand:

- that transparency in the communication process is essential to building trust
- that persuasion requires preparation
- that persuasion takes time

How to suggest the way forward to your Ex

When Douglas Stone and his colleagues published *Difficult Conversations,* it quickly became a bestseller because the book met a need.[44] Generally, people were neither confident nor effective in having sensitive conversations.

Douglas Stone's advice resonates as strongly today as it did when first published in 2000.

There are many types of difficult conversations you have to have throughout your life. Few discussions are more sensitive than those during the process of separation, especially if trust of the other party is elusive and irritation and anger are simmering. The task of persuading your Ex of the way forward is a tricky prospect. Handle this task badly, and delay and obstruction may await you. Handle it well, and you will skilfully contribute to building respect and cooperation during a sensitive process. This chapter spotlights factors which can be useful when the time comes to persuade your Ex of the most constructive, inexpensive and expedient way to legally finalise your separation.

Discussing with your Ex your preferred separation legal pathway first relies on you being informed and confident that the option you have identified is the best way forward. Are you fully informed? Why is it the best option for you? Your former partner?

How would you go about suggesting the option you think might work best for finalising matters? What will you say? How will you say it? It is important to think about this. Write down what you want to say. Now read it out aloud. How does it sound? Read it out aloud to a trusted friend or advisor to get some feedback. Is what you say persuasive? Respectful? What opposition might your Ex have to your suggestions? Does your separation situation lend itself to conversations during which you can raise options and identify advantages? If it is likely that your Ex will respond favourably, this potentially makes the case for a cooperative process like mediation or collaborative law. The way you go about persuading your Ex that your preferred option is the one that will work best for you both —is, in short, *crucial.*

Your preparation should include consideration of the issues which typify your circumstances, your personalities, the demands on each of you, and the time and expense involved. The use of gentle language which sensitively appraises the facts to be considered will have the greatest chance of success with your

Ex. This applies to any method of communication—in person, telephone, email, letter, FaceTime, Zoom, Skype or other conferencing technology. The key is to present as *neutral* in your assessment of your preferred option.

Be wary of the strong differences between face-to-face interactions and communication by email and text. Using email has risks. While it can be an efficient way to communicate, the content of emails can readily be misunderstood, especially because email is not a conversation in which statements can be clarified and intentions understood. Email is not 'an emotion-free zone'. It can easily lead to conflict.[45]

And if you think picking up the telephone is devoid of problems, think again. As a way of communicating, the telephone is less problematic than email. But according to Douglas Stone, 'the phone conveys tone of voice ... it does not convey facial expressions. That makes understanding subtle emotions and meaning tougher. You hear the other person complaining, but you don't see the vulnerability and sadness in their eyes'.[46] Openly voicing empathy and understanding the stress that your Ex may be experiencing can be useful.

Part of your preparation is collecting information. Why not include some brochures about collaborative law or mediation, or both? Can you also mention some useful websites which provide information about the legal pathway you prefer? The advantages of providing your Ex with these sources of information are, first, that these sources are independent of you; and second, that the information can be discussed between you both so that you are both working from the same page.

Rehearsing your approach can be valuable. If your approach is face-to-face, whether in person or via technology, why not rehearse with a trusted friend first? Rehearsing will help you become more articulate and give a smoother presentation. Rehearsing will also help you get your tone right and prevent you from coming across as condescending or controlling or confused about the benefits of the option you are recommending. It will help you make sure that you address all the relevant points in your proposal.

These are respectful steps that will foster progress to the conclusion of your legal pathway.

Tips for Approaching your Ex

Prepare	Talk through your approach with a trusted advisor. Learn about what is involved in each option, and the advantages and limitations of each option.
Identify advantages / limitations of options	Identify the advantages for each of you. Be neutral in your coverage of these and seek your Ex's views on each of the options. Help your Ex feel that their views matter. But do not overwhelm them with information. This may arouse suspicion, irritation or resentment.
Be flexible	Inform your Ex that you are willing to consider their suggestions. Whatever you do, avoid appearing to dictate the terms of the option to be taken. The most *damaging* communication of all is to tell your Ex what to do. Flexibility can inject a tone of teamwork to 'get the separation done and dusted'. Why not consider phrases such as 'I have read through the literature on this option and it seems that the advantages outweigh the disadvantages. This seems the cheaper option for us both. I'm keen to know what *you* think.'
Be respectful	Use neutral language that is not condescending or threatening.
Persist	Your Ex may at first decline to consider your approach at all. They may be prepared to reconsider your suggestion after having had time to digest further the information you have provided, and assessed the advantages and limitations for themselves, given their new (separated) circumstances.

But then again, it's not that simple for everyone. If the situation requires it you can simply go straight to your lawyer and begin lawyer-assisted negotiation. Remember to take charge, provide clear instructions to your lawyer about the tone, limits and substance of the correspondence you expect between your lawyer and the lawyer representing your Ex. Details of your working relationship with your lawyer will be discussed in section five.

Conclusion

Delicate conversations are not easy. Consideration of the sensitivities of your former partner, will be an ongoing factor until the legal formalities of separation are finalised. Moreso, if children are involved.

This chapter has addressed the challenges of persuading your former partner of the most fruitful way forward. The chapter has shown you how to avoid mistakes and take positive, constructive steps to achieve your goal. Remember, move forward with purpose and, if your former partner needs a little guidance in doing so, model resolve and fairness.

8
Using questions, silence, and listening skills

This chapter provides you with an overview of strategic communication skills, such as asking questions, using silence, and actively listening during your separation deliberations with your Ex. Earlier in this book you will have noted that the most common reason couples cite for ending their relationship, besides money, is 'lack of communication'. If this has been a relevant factor in your separation, then now is the time to try to improve your skills so that you can finalise your separation productively. Of course, these skills can only be applied if your situation permits.

This chapter offers you opportunities to understand:

- the structure and uses of questions and silence
- the mechanics of listening
- how to critically observe the behaviour of your former partner

Questions

Questions play an essential role in your separation process, especially the division of assets. Asking 'Why?' is one of the most important actions you can take in understanding the interests of your Ex. When you ask 'Why?' you seek to understand where they are coming from. Questions can set the tone of the discussion as well as elicit information. Demonstrate to your Ex that you are listening with the purpose of genuinely understanding what is important to them. Try asking, 'What is your basic concern here for [wanting this]?'. Asking 'Why not?' ensures that you think more critically about your Ex's choice. Let's explore this further.

In their pathbreaking book, *Getting to Yes,* negotiation experts, Roger Fisher and William Ury, advocate a useful way to identify the other party's interests.[47] First, you need to identify the decision that you have asked your Ex to make, and second, ask yourself why your Ex has not made that decision. What underlies their interests? You need to be thinking on your feet here. You need to be alert to what your Ex says and doesn't say—what they ask for and what they do not ask for. While your settlement discussions will largely be financial in nature, Fisher and Ury contend that the most powerful interests are basic human needs. [48] When you are trying to identify the interests of your Ex, you need to be mindful of the fundamental needs that most people tend to have: security, economic wellbeing, a sense of belonging, recognition, and control over one's life. If you keep this in mind, you will be well placed to reach agreement. But these factors only work for people who are prepared to be reasonable.

The bargaining you will be conducting is known as 'interest based bargaining'. Interest based bargaining allows negotiators to look for creative solutions.[49] To do this, you need to volunteer information and ask a lot of questions, focus on the interests and goals you have in common, trade assets you care about less for things that matter to you more, and think of yourself and the other negotiator (your Ex) as partners in problem solving—provided your relationship situation allows for this. In a negotiation, you and your Ex have common goals as well as conflicting ones. Conflicting goals often stand out. If you and your Ex focus too intently on how goals conflict, you may miss where your interests intersect.

Asking questions is often incorrectly thought to be a weakness in negotiation. Even if you have known your Ex intimately for many years, there may be times during negotiation when you do not know what they want. You might not know their motivations for the positions they take in the negotiation. The wisest move then is to ask for this information. Fisher and Ury explain this process in detail.[50] They contend that asking the question 'Why?' is about two things. The first is about looking backwards for a cause of the dilemma, and treats your behaviour as determined by prior events. The second looks forward for a purpose and treats your behaviour as subject to free will. It is your choice whether you look backwards or forwards, but your negotiation will be far more effective if you discuss the direction in which you want to go. You are advised to *best leave the past alone*, however hard that may be for you. Instead, discuss what you would like to see happen in the future.

To avoid non-cooperation set some ground rules for bargaining before you start. If you give information and you find that your former partner is not giving anything away, establish a standard of reciprocity for information sharing. For bargaining to work the discussion must be mutual. Be direct about this.

Try to ask your questions in an open-ended way that does not leave your former partner with the only option of a closed answer. Skip questions which invite yes/no answers. Ask them an open-ended question. Perhaps you could try asking, 'What are your reactions to what I have suggested?' Or, 'How does that sit with you?' If your Ex's responses are forthcoming in a low conflict environment, they will likely provide you with the information you need.

If asking open-ended questions does not get your Ex to open up, then try asking non-threatening questions to push them a little to open up. However, be careful not to be condescending. If the negotiation about possessions or a certain item proves to be a sticking point, then why not ask your former partner something non-threatening like, 'It seems to me that giving me the stereo is something that is really unacceptable to you. But I am not sure why. Can you please tell me why?' Or why not something like, 'Of all the items we co-own, the house is the most important to me to keep. What items are more important to you? Why don't we tell each other what our most important items are?' If your Ex answers and starts to open up, then this neutral position has achieved positive progress.

Show a willingness to share information and explanations. This can influence the other party to respond in kind even if they have different positions on a number of issues.

Ask your Ex what they want, why they want it, why they think what they want is fair, and why they think their solution is better than any other option. Asking for information (and getting it) is essential to your ability to bargain. Seeking information will *not* leave you open to exploitation. Avoid doing what others mistakenly do by being tight-lipped and secretive. Asking questions is one of the fundamental techniques of cooperative bargaining—*asking questions and listening carefully to the answers.*

What is really important here, admittedly in amicable situations, is not just cooperation, but letting your Ex know that you care about *their priorities* and that together you can sort matters out. Knowing more about the priorities of your Ex will also contribute to identifying areas which are *not* problematic. It narrows the list of items which both of you want so that you can begin to bargain. If you actively listen and ask for their point of view, you will avoid being seen as adversarial.

When you approach your negotiation prepared to bargain cooperatively, you can achieve positive outcomes. Such outcomes can include reducing the cost of your legal fees and a more rewarding property settlement for you. It can lower your stress levels. It can foster effective decision-making. And, if you have children, it can assist them to adjust to change.

And while careful and sensitive communication is the order of the day, *be sure to sense when your efforts are not working and it is best to simply walk away.* There are always other options.

Ways to use silence

Silence can be a very useful technique in separation negotiations.[51] When you are negotiating your property settlement for instance, silence can be a valuable ally during face-to-face bargaining.

There are four types of silence which the great negotiators use which you can draw on in your bargaining: attentive silence; wise silence; 'second chance' silence; and challenging silence.[52] Learning more about silence, the types of silence, and how to listen to silence (including what is not said) can bolster your armoury of communication techniques. Understanding and practising them is well worth your time.

1. The attentive silence

Attentive silence requires you to show your Ex that you are listening actively to what they are saying, taking in what they say, and considering it with the respect it deserves. When practising and applying this skill, try looking at your Ex and nod your head now and again. Doing this invites trust and will encourage them to tell you more. This is not wielding a skill to exploit the other person. When you use silence that is attentive and respectful, the other person will often tell you more than they intended. You may be able to use silence to progress the negotiation further to its completion.

2. The wise silence

The wise silence typically involves you pausing with deliberation before you respond to a difficult question posed by your Ex. Skilled negotiators typically use this pause to gain control of the conversation. For example, deliberate over a point the other party has just raised. Appear thoughtful. Turn the exchange in the direction you think will be productive to outcomes by asking for clarity on issues before you can give an answer to their question.

3. The 'second chance' silence

The second chance silence typically involves you giving your Ex an opportunity to clarify what they have just told you. Deliver your silence with a direct and unflinching gaze, with a facial expression that indicates expectation (rather than approval/criticism). What this tactic does is to implicitly pressure the other party to provide more detail with the intent of making concessions.

4. The challenging silence

The challenging silence requires you to stay silent when the situation is deadlocked and neither you nor your Ex wants to concede or give ground in any way. Both you and your Ex may feel that the first to speak weakens your own position. If you find yourself in this situation, prolong the silence and then break the silence by saying, for example, 'You are a determined negotiator. How do you propose to proceed?'.

Which one, or combination, of these types of silences appeal to you and your situation? Practise these techniques until you have refined them. Once refined to the point of being applied with ease, adding the power of sharp listening skills will make you a more astute communicator than ever before. Outcomes you seek will come your way.

Combining questions, silence and listening makes for a powerful armoury of communication. Let's explore the skill of listening.

Listening skills

New York Times journalist Kate Murphy has interviewed professional listeners from spies to hostage negotiators and all those in between. In her book, *You're Not Listening*, she argues that listening goes beyond hearing someone speak to note the *manner* and *context* in which people speak. She says that effective listening depends on the skill with which the listener can draw out the speaker's thoughts through questions and curiosity. Effective listening can enrich the way you experience the world.[53]

Talented negotiators have certain qualities in common: an outstanding capacity for listening; observing; and spotting details. While I am not suggesting that you become a world-class negotiator overnight, these skills will make a positive difference to any sensitive discussion, especially if you appreciate the value of questions and silence.

If you are keen to develop and improve your ability to listen and observe, it would be wise for you to learn the three levels of listening which will strengthen your ability to read the different signals that the other party sends out. The three levels of listening refer to listening for meaning, intention and emotions.[54]

1. Listening for meaning

Listening for meaning requires you to listen to the immediate meaning of your Ex's words. A lot of the time, in the midst of a robust discussion, it is difficult to accurately identify the meaning of the other person's words. The only way of ensuring you understand the intended meaning is to try to periodically rephrase the essence of what you have just heard. For instance, 'In other words, you really want to see the children once a month on a Saturday?' Or, 'So, what you are really saying is that outing me at work is your way of explaining that, due to your personal life, you are not on top of your game?'

2. Listening for intentions

Listening for intentions requires you to understand what is *behind* the immediate meaning of the words—what the other person is trying to get you to understand or to believe. Is there a deeper meaning to what your former partner is saying to you? What is the effect on you? Be alert to underlying intentions.

3. Listening for emotions

Listening for emotions requires you to be alert to the underlying emotions of your Ex when they make claims, ask questions or present proposals. If, during a negotiation, your former partner claims that what you are proposing is utterly ridiculous, the important thing here is to keep in mind the person's state of mind. Does their blunt remark express a feeling of irritation, anger, hurt, unease, a genuine sense of unfairness, or is it simply the destructive pleasure of revenge-based bargaining?

Is there an art to listening?

Of the communication skills you learn in your developmental growth, you learn first to listen, you learn second to speak, you learn third to read, and you learn fourth to write.[55] Despite this primacy of learning to listen as your first developmental milestone, listening is the communication skill least taught. Surprisingly, given the significance of listening, parents and educators do not teach children how to listen well.

What is 'good listening'?

Good listening is the active, disciplined kind of listening that drives you to examine and challenge the information you hear in order to improve its quality and quantity, and thereby improve your decision-making. It is pivotal to gaining insights, developing ideas and innovation.[56]

The importance of listening cannot be emphasised too greatly. During the separation process, listening actively is one of the smartest things you can do. When you listen actively, you help create a mutually engaging conversation. When it involves an exchange of information, listening actively ensures that the discussion is goal-oriented and productive.

How would you describe your own listening habits? How would you describe the listening habits of your former partner? Do these listening habits change? In stressful situations? It is worth reviewing your own listening habits so that you can audit your listening strengths and weaknesses and correct them for use when communicating during the separation process. Why not complete the following exercise to review your listening behaviours? And be honest about this. No one's looking over your shoulder!

Review your listening habits

Please tick the following behaviours which resonate with you.

- ☐ No matter what the speaker says, you bring the topic back to yourself.
- ☐ You respond to what the speaker says by negating what they say.
- ☐ You do not respond to what is being said to you, either verbally or via body language.
- ☐ You switch off if it is not something you want to hear.
- ☐ You interrupt and talk over the top of the speaker.
- ☐ You pretend to pay attention when you are not.
- ☐ You try to do other things while listening.

- ☐ You decide the subject is uninteresting.
- ☐ You get distracted by the speaker's way of speech or other mannerisms.
- ☐ You get over-involved and thus lose the main thread of the arguments or thoughts.
- ☐ You let emotion-filled words arouse your personal anger and antagonism.
- ☐ You doodle, fiddle or rearrange yourself while only half-listening.
- ☐ You are 'going through the motions'.
- ☐ You concentrate on any distraction instead of what is being said.
- ☐ You listen primarily for the facts.
- ☐ You avoid anything that is emotionally or intellectually complex or difficult.

How many of these behaviours did you tick? Think about this for a moment. Why did you tick the answers you did? Consider how these qualities impact on your interactions with others. Think especially about your most sensitive interactions with your Ex and your lawyer. Could you listen better? If you demonstrated active listening skills, would you receive much more information than you do? To paraphrase the words of revered philosopher Dr Maya Angelou, 'Few may remember what you said, but everyone will remember how you made them feel'. Review your listening habits. Review them often. Listen and show respect to others.

Effective actions

There are some practical actions which, together, comprise the 'art' of listening. Taking these actions will not only enable you to listen as well as 'hear' what your former partner has to say, but to *make them feel listened to.* This will place you closer to achieving the outcomes that you are seeking.

The following list provides you with several of the key techniques to help improve your listening skills.

Focus

Practise tuning out distracting noises. An active focus on who and what you are listening to puts this process into effect. You will get more value from your interaction, especially if you are seeking a relationship separation outcome.

The 80:20 rule and the value of demonstrated respect

Communication experts argue that you should listen 80% of the time and talk only 20%. This will come as a bit of a shock to some people, but why not try it? There are various ways to use your 20%. You can simply express your views in a manner that reflects that you have been actively listening to your Ex. You can use your 20% to ask questions about issues your Ex has raised. These decisions depend on the purpose of the conversation and the importance of their consequences.

No interrupting

Interrupting and talking over the top of someone is utterly offensive. It immediately conveys that what *you* have to say is far more important than what the other person has to say. It is even more offensive when the other person is struggling to express themselves about an issue they find difficult. Interrupting them is not helping. Even if you find the progress of discussions excruciatingly slow, even if you think you have heard it twenty times before, even if you know the other party is mistaken, do *not* interrupt. Patience is required, so let pauses and short periods of silence be. Interrupting is the fastest way to convey to the other person that they are not being listened to — that you have absolutely no interest at all in listening to them. Interrupting and talking over the top of your former partner can damage the bargaining process. Resentment can build into insurmountable obstacles with any belief in your sincerity evaporating.

Being respectful to the other person means letting them know that you are interested in what they have to say; that their views are as important as yours. You can do this by asking questions which let your Ex know that you have heard what they have said—and not by criticising what they have said. You can also do this through the use of affirmation. Use body language like a nod and a 'vocal nod' or listening phrase like 'I hear you' or even 'mmm hmm' or 'uh hum' to confirm to the other party that you are listening and are with them every step of the way.

Body talk and eye contact

Being able to interpret body language matters to the outcomes you can achieve from listening. Observing the other person's body language tells you more than the words being spoken. It tells you about deception, sincerity, priorities, and emotions. While observation can tell *you* about how the other person is feeling, your *own* body language reveals things about you, more than the words you speak. Your body language impacts on how the other person perceives you and what you are saying. Reflect on your past relationship with your Ex. Describe your body language during sensitive discussions. Now reverse this reflective task. Describe the body language of your former partner during sensitive discussions and during arguments. If you react negatively to what the other person is saying, your body language will reveal this and likely inhibit the willingness of your Ex to continue talking to you. Be aware of this. Maintain a relaxed but respectful composure.

Eye contact is important in showing the other person that you are listening. Let them know that they have your attention. Lean slightly forward to demonstrate that you are interested in what they have to say. Slight turns of the head at the right time also tell the other person that you are actively listening to them. Reflecting or mirroring the expressions of the speaker to demonstrate empathy also conveys your engagement. Do not doodle, fidget or otherwise engage in distracting physical gestures while the other person is talking. It is too obvious that your attention does not reside with the speaker. This will not help you achieve your outcomes. It will only serve to irritate.

Content and validation

Content matters. Focus on the *content* of what your Ex is saying. Do *not* be distracted or judge hastily the way your Ex is expressing their thoughts. There are other factors such as nervousness, hurt, distress or anger which may be in play when you or your Ex are trying to express yourselves during settlement negotiations. Were there any recurring contentious issues during your relationship? Might they present during your parenting or property division bargaining? Focusing on *content and context* rather than just the facts at hand helps you 'connect the dots' of the issues your Ex is talking about.

When it is appropriate to do so, openly validate the view that your Ex has just expressed. Try to overcome any sense of discomfort, indignation or anxiety at their distress. Ramp up how actively you are listening to them. If they are upset about an issue, let them know that you can appreciate that they are upset and understand the reasons why. Make sure you let them say everything that they want to say. Empathy is important at times when your former partner is upset, disappointed, angry, frustrated, hurt or distressed. It is far more important to let your former partner know that you understand than it is to tell them what they need to do or offer solutions. Focus. Get the results you seek.

Conclusion

Practise your skills in as many social situations as you can. Do not be afraid to ask people for feedback. Do they think you are a good listener? What happens when you use silence in some everyday situations? What do you notice? Deliberately ask questions in conversations to discover more about the person you are talking to. Questioning, silence, and listening are skills that will enrich your life. Be genuine. Make them part of the way you engage with people. Yes, separation is stressful and engaging with people with genuine curiosity while you are stressed can be taxing. Visualise applying these skills successfully in your separation bargaining. Practice will lead to good results for you.

9

Stand your ground: Assertiveness

The previous chapter covered the importance of the skilful use of questions, silence and listening in your communication with your Ex. This chapter extends your communication skillset to include assertiveness. You will need to be constantly aware of how to express yourself in a way that conveys to your Ex that you are firm in your decisions and will not tolerate obstruction or any other wrongdoing.

This chapter offers you opportunities to understand:

- the big picture of assertiveness
- strategies for improving your own assertiveness
- how to apply assertive communication strategies

Boundaries

Boundaries are so very important in making, communicating and implementing your decisions. During your separation process, establishing boundaries for communication will be very important from the outset. You and your Ex may have previously done well to establish some boundaries about acceptable behaviours, but your separation suggests that these boundaries have deteriorated. Making decisions about what you want for yourself, without having to consider your Ex, involves setting identifiable boundaries of what you want and don't want, what you will accept and what you won't accept, etc. Thus, boundaries are important for shaping your life, including your future.

Boundary-setting during settlement bargaining is best done sensitively, but it will be necessary to express your refusal to accept disrespectful conduct. This is not directing a criticism at your Ex. It is setting a boundary of behaviour you will not accept. Be specific in identifying the behaviour. Ensure that you avoid accusatory language. Talk about the behaviour, not the person. Name the behaviour. If you want to develop this, you can identify the behaviour that you would prefer, e.g. 'What I would like to see happen is ...', 'I would appreciate it if you would ...' or 'I find that unacceptable...' or 'Your anger is not helping...'. Understanding where your Ex is coming from will help you shape your comments to ask for action by the other person. For example, 'I know you don't enjoy doing it, but the children need you to be at the parent–teacher conference this Friday. I will meet you outside the front gate at 3 pm.' Another example, 'I would appreciate your continued discretion about my sexuality. My work and home life are separate. I want to keep it that way.'

Boundaries and assertiveness go hand in hand. Assertiveness fuels your ability to express your views firmly and clearly and, in the process, establish boundaries which protect the integrity of the way you live your life. Its importance merits exploration, so let's take a look at assertive communication and the qualities it comprises.

What is assertiveness?

Assertiveness is defined as 'direct, honest and appropriate ways of standing up for your rights while respecting the rights of others'.[57] Learning and strengthening this skill as soon as you can will strengthen your bargaining ability and boost your confidence. It can improve your wellbeing and the way you engage with others generally. Your assertiveness skills will improve with practice. When things do not go as well as you had hoped, reflect on what you *could* have said and how you could have replied so you can respond more effectively next time. Rehearse and apply these skills in a variety of situations. If you do not have a trusted friend or family member to role-play with, then use the mirror. In this, you are not alone. Many people use this technique.

How many of you have been in relationship situations where you have not stood up for yourself? Allowed others to put their needs before yours? Allowed them to 'walk over the top of you'? For many, the devastating consequence of just 'taking it' is diminished self-respect, accumulated resentment and low self-esteem—that sense of being a 'doormat'. Evan Stark's book *Coercive Control* is highly relevant here and merits your reading.[58] If your self-respect has diminished over time, resentment will likely undermine your ability to live your life with confidence. To others, your inability to be assertive can be expressed as aggression. If you're not assertive, you may also be a conflict avoider. To avoid conflict, you allow others to violate your boundaries and dismiss your rights and feelings. In turn, you retain a seething, but subtly expressed resentment, or feeling of 'dying inside'.

There is good news, however. Assertiveness can be learned.

Ways to build your assertiveness

Let's explore some useful ways you can build your assertiveness skills. You may like to practise these in conjunction with your listening skills. This time listen to yourself.

Control your breathing

Focus on controlling your breathing. Try to maintain regular breathing rather than short breaths, or worse, suspending your breathing if you are someone who freezes with panic. When you practise your assertive communication techniques, practise your breathing as well. Breathe evenly and calmly. Assertiveness is not just about speaking and drawing boundaries, it can also be about silence. Remember, you do *not* have to speak until you are ready, whether you are in your lawyer's office or bargaining with your Ex. You will know when you are ready to speak because your ability to be calm and think clearly will return. For some, this return to calmness may take longer than others. If this is the case, consider telling your lawyer or your Ex that you will get back to them when you have thought the matter through. This, in itself, is assertive conduct. Demonstrate that you treat *yourself* with respect.

Be clear

Try to express your point of view clearly, using direct language. If you're talking to your Ex there are some phrases to avoid. For instance, do your best to avoid undermining your message with passive qualifiers like 'It isn't that important to me, but ...' or 'That's if you don't mind ...' or 'I am happy to do that, but ...'. A passive communication style simply serves to shoot yourself in the foot and irritate the other party. Summon up the courage to make it known what you really think to make sure the other person knows exactly what you mean. If it helps, have points written down in front of you.

Use your voice

Try to speak in an even but firm tone, one that can be heard clearly. *How* you say what you want to say is just as important as *what* you say. Firmness will support the clarity of your message. Speaking quietly or hesitatingly will not help you. A firm manner on your part will help prevent any potential bullying from your Ex and/or their representatives.

Body language

Whether you are talking to your lawyer or your Ex, your body language matters. Try to ensure that your body language matches what you are saying. If you are expressing your point of view, look the other person in the eye, stand up/sit up straight with feet firmly planted, relax your shoulders and use a relaxed facial expression. You may find that repeatedly practising this exercise with a friend will help you develop confidence with this aspect of your communication. Your friend can give you feedback on how you present yourself. Using contradictory body language will be confusing and annoying to the other party. Looking at the ground will not help your case. Nor will looking at the sky!

Stick to the facts

When you express your point of view, draw on *factual* information and observation rather than judgement. The credibility of the information is an important issue, especially if your Ex is hostile to anything you have to say. Why not tell your Ex the source of your facts? Maintaining an even tone, neutral language and a neutral facial expression will be useful to your assertive presentation.

Use 'I' statements

This is a tried and true assertiveness communication technique which involves staying away from accusatory 'you' language. Using the phrases, 'I feel this when you do that ...', 'I think' and 'I feel' is typical of this approach. For instance, try, 'When you are late picking up the children I feel frustrated. I would appreciate it if you could try to be on time.' Or, 'When you attend the same book club as me I feel uncomfortable and unable to participate. Let's agree to attend different sessions. I feel that would be healthy for both of us.' This technique focuses on the personal position to voice one's thoughts rather than the judgemental position, and on avoiding blaming the other person for how you feel.

What to do when things escalate

Regrettably, many of you will probably encounter situations in which you need to impress upon your Ex that a need has not been addressed, despite repeated attempts to do so. This requires you to be *firmer* as you attempt to have the issue resolved. In the face of non-cooperation or obstruction it may require you to identify a consequence. For instance, 'This is the fifth time you have been late with child support. I have tried to explain how difficult this makes things for me, but you seem not to respect this. I am aware that you are able to make these payments, but you choose not to. If you are late again, I will lodge a formal complaint and you know that will have consequences that you won't like.' Or, if in a same-sex relationship, 'I do not appreciate you badmouthing me to our mutual friends. Stop it. It is not respectful behaviour'. You have a right to take reasonable actions so take them.

Control your emotions

If you are intimidated, upset, hurt or angry it is hard to express yourself clearly. Try to control your breathing, use an even tone of voice and focus on what you need to say. *Use your focus as your instrument of self-control.* Should you be in a mediation or collaborative law process situation, you will have options to manage this without inflaming the situation. Remember chapter two's discussion of anger which results in shooting yourself in the foot? If you need time to get your emotions under control, try saying, 'Just give me a moment, please' or 'I will get back to you on that'. There is a lot to be said for keeping your head. Maintaining evenness in difficult situations may take a little practice. But once you feel yourself improving your self-esteem grows and self-confidence energises your determination to improve your assertiveness skills. Besides, letting your emotions rule you will cost you money in more legal fees; money that you need for your future. There is a saying: 'Think financially, not emotionally'. Heed this.

How to deal with criticism

Throughout your separation process you may receive criticism from your Ex. It may come directly from your Ex, depending on the legal process you choose, or it may come via correspondence from your Ex's lawyer. These remarks will sting. It is possible, however, to deal effectively with criticism. Being assertive in the face of criticism *is* possible. And the more you practise this, the better you will handle criticism from your Ex.

There can be a range of reasons why your Ex may be throwing criticisms at you during the separation process. Try to think whether the criticism being levelled at you is really about the issue being mentioned or whether there is another factor in play. It may even be as simple as mere frustration on the part of your Ex regarding new arrangements that are time consuming. It may be that they have had a bad day. Let them know that you have heard them and reflect on their criticism. This helps ensure that the point they are trying to get across (however negatively) is understood by you. If the criticism has a kernel of truth to it, acknowledge this, no matter how uncomfortable this may be. Whatever you do, avoid throwing criticism back at your former partner. This is destructive to your interests. Do not return their negative or aggressive communication.

Be better than this, if only for your sake.

Useful phrases to help you think on your feet

Have useful assertive phrases on hand. Practise saying these phrases and think about some of the situations you might have experienced where these phrases might have come in handy for you. Some of these phrases include:

- 'No, thank you.'
- 'I could use some help.'
- 'Please do not speak to me like that.'
- 'No, I have other plans.'
- 'I would like your support with this.'
- 'I'm just not comfortable with that.'
- 'I do not want a future with you.'
- 'This option serves the best interests of our children because ...'
- 'My views are just as important as yours.'
- 'I want to keep the house because ...'
- 'Our children need you not to bad-mouth me because it hurts them.'
- 'I hear what you are saying, though I disagree.'

Conclusion

Standing your ground requires *assertiveness.* This is a skill which is so very important during the process of finalising the legal aspects of your separation. The good news is that assertiveness can not only be learned it can be improved. With it comes an empowering boost to your self-confidence. This will change your life and serve you well in all areas of life far beyond your separation process.

SECTION 4
LEGAL PATHWAYS

10

Options for your legal process

This chapter is the first in the section which discusses the legal options available to you for your separation. The array of pathways you will be able to choose from include: Court-based litigation, arbitration, 'unbundling', Do-It-Yourself, lawyer-assisted negotiation, mediation, and the collaborative law process. Each of these pathways have different legal costs issues. Of course, the option you choose will depend on the level of conflict between you and your Ex. It is essential that you know as much as you can about the legal pathways for dissolving your relationship so that you can make an informed decision.

This chapter offers you opportunities to understand:

- that there are options available to you to legally end your relationship
- the overview of each option of litigation, arbitration, unbundling, DIY, kitchen table negotiations, round table conferences
- that there are advantages and disadvantages for you to weigh in choosing your pathway

Options

Litigation: Court

Many people have horror stories about their experience with the Court system: that it feels like they are on another planet; that there are language and rules and representations of their separation situation that barely resemble the realities of their experience. Things are even more difficult for people whose first language is not English even when they are provided with an interpreter.

In Australia, the Court system of separation involves the two primary courts: The Magistrates Court and the Federal Circuit and Family Court of Australia (the Court). There is an abundance of research and anecdotal evidence which says that taking your matter to Court is very expensive, drawn out and mostly unsatisfactory. This process can take years to complete and will swallow the resources you need for your future. In many countries even getting into Court is a drawn-out process.

By going to Court, your separation situation will be drastically reduced to a set of facts deemed relevant only to the Court. And what's more, control of any decision-making is taken out of your hands. The decision is handed down *long* after you enter the process and after you have spent way more than, say, the minimum AUS $50,000 (and in many cases that amount is on the low side). It can lead you to exhaustion. It can waste years of your life. Taking your matter to Court will envelop you in a period of prolonged high stress and diminished wellbeing. During this period stress-related illness is common. And the people closest to you will wear the burden of your angst.

Now you know why ethical lawyers and past clients say, 'Avoid Court at all costs. Deal. Trade-off. Bargain. Decide what you can live with. Do it now. Focus on your future.'

Arbitration

Arbitration is a process that is essentially a private arrangement. It provides an alternative to a decision by a judge. This can be less expensive than other options and more efficient in terms of time. Arbitration is an option available only in circumstances that do not involve children. During the process of arbitration, the two parties submit their documentation to the arbitrator, who is typically a lawyer, and are subject to the arbitrator's determination of the outcome. This option affords the former partners a greater measure of privacy. This is an especially appealing feature when it comes to high-profile individuals.

Be mindful of the legalities of the arbitration option, however. The decision will not be legally binding until it is registered by the Court. Like other options, there are grounds upon which the Court can set aside arbitration decisions. For instance, the presence of fraud, unconscionable conduct, and other factors which undermine the integrity of the arbitration process. There are obviously more complexities to the arbitration option than mentioned here. Be sure to consult your family lawyer to gain more detail.

'Step in Step Out' / 'Unbundling'

You do some tasks. Your lawyer does some tasks. But be wary of this option because if you do not complete the tasks correctly they will need to be redone which means more expense. And never lose sight of the fact that your lawyer knows way more than you do about the application of the law. 'Unbundling' is also referred to as 'step-in-step-out', 'discrete legal task services' or 'limited scope representation'. Unbundling is suited to straightforward matters not involving child custody disputes or contest of any kind.

Need a closer picture of what unbundling looks like? It operates this way: you meet with your lawyer and provide all the necessary information. Your lawyer assesses the information to ensure your case is appropriate for the unbundled option and the possible outcomes of select actions to be taken. You and your lawyer draw up an agreement which details the tasks you will do and which tasks your lawyer will do. Your lawyer will provide you with a fixed cost to offer you price certainty and will give you an idea of the timeframe in which they will complete the work. Be sure that you understand the scope of the agreement between you and your lawyer, and that you are completely clear about what your lawyer will and will not be doing. You will be deeply involved in monitoring the progress of your matter so make sure your personal circumstances allow you the time to do this.

DIY: Do it yourself legal work

The number of people who are opting for completing many of the tasks in the legal process themselves is increasing. Be sure to have your lawyer examine your final paperwork so that you avoid costly mistakes or risk having your paperwork returned for correction. You will be required to document that you have consulted the advice of an independent lawyer (depending on your state/country of residence).

Also, other informal negotiations can take place between former partners in amicable circumstances. There are now online forms, DIY Divorce Kits, and brief courses available that make it easier for people to complete their legal separation process independent of lawyers. This innovation has occurred in the context of increased client education, a distaste for expensive legal fees, and a perception of a lack of transparency in the provision of legal services. There are still certain legal fees which apply to the administration of this process and the processing of the documents involved.

This option, though the least expensive, is not for everyone. I urge you not to go down this path without first consulting a lawyer and then having a lawyer review your documentation. There are a number of reasons for this: you could miss important points that could save you considerable costs, deprive you of much-needed resources, and have other significant consequences down the track. Never assume you know more than an experienced family lawyer. DIY kits might make the process seem easier, but they don't come with years of experience or an in-depth knowledge from a lawyer's extensive understanding of the law.

Assessing Kitchen Table Negotiation

Do not take the term 'kitchen table' literally. It is a term which merely indicates a lack of legal formality. It is a discussion between you and your former spouse—without your lawyers present. All going well, this option can save you and your Ex lots of money. But it can only be achieved if both former partners can directly negotiate amicably. Key factors which make this option possible for you and your Ex are that both parties:

- have a basic understanding of the family law system
- have a thorough understanding of the legal consequences of your decisions
- have a determination to maintain cooperation and respect for the other

- possess sound and focused emotional stability
- possess the skills to communicate effectively
- maintain equality of power and transparency.

After issues have been agreed upon, the paperwork needs to be formally drawn up by your family lawyer in order for the agreement to be legally binding. It is especially important to keep your lawyer involved when it comes to financial matters to prevent mistakes which can have nasty consequences. In any case, it is a good idea to keep consulting your family lawyer, even if it is just to make sure things are on track.

Do not agree to anything until you have spoken to your family lawyer.

'Kitchen table' negotiations are typically not completed in one sitting. Negotiations may take several weeks or even months. Be careful to avoid being idealistic about this option. It is rare for tension to be absent from any discussion regarding the allocation of finances and care for children.

Let's take a look at the benefits of kitchen table negotiations in order to inform your choice of legal pathways for your separation. [59]

Assessing kitchen table negotiation

Advantages	Disadvantages
Minimal cost due to limited involvement from professional advisors.	Can lead to conflict if you and your Ex are not able to communicate calmly.
You and your Ex control the negotiation, so it can be done quite quickly.	Can be risky if you are not first aware of your legal rights and entitlements, and perhaps are led into an agreement that is not entirely appropriate for you.
If you and your Ex are able to agree on small issues it will assist in developing a strong parenting relationship in the future.	If the agreement is not formalised there may be legal and financial risks that arise in the future that you are not aware of right now.

Round table conference / Without prejudice conference

Both 'round table' and 'without prejudice' conference refer to another lawyer-assisted negotiation option. The 'round table conference' is deemed 'without prejudice' because the contents of the discussion cannot be used against either party in Court. The limits to such an arrangement are determined by the level of conflict between former partners.

What is a 'round table conference'? It is a conference or, if the matter is complex, a series of conferences, in which you and your Ex meet for discussions to resolve issues such as parenting arrangements and the division of property. In these circumstances, former partners in low conflict communication can sit with their lawyers at the same table, different rooms, or locations using conferencing technology to resolve issues. One or the other lawyer will open discussions and both lawyers should have with them all relevant information and documentation (discussed in chapter five) regarding your separation.[60]

The advantage exists when conflict is low, communication clear, and lawyers are deft in legal bargaining and behave in a balanced fashion (rather than one lawyer being unduly aggressive). In a positive scenario, decisions can be reached quickly.

However, be mindful of the need to apply the advice of your financial advisor/counsellor, should the situation require it. And remember to prepare. Make sure you know who will be present, that the necessary documents have been reviewed, and that you are clear about the outcomes you are seeking.

Conclusion

While I have provided this information to show you your pathways and save money on legal fees, I have chosen to explore in greater detail the options of lawyer-assisted negotiation, mediation, and the collaborative law process in the next three chapters. Self-driven methods have their limitations.

11
Lawyer-assisted negotiation

The purpose of this chapter is to familiarise you with the option of lawyer-assisted negotiation via correspondence. Knowing more about the pros and cons of this particular pathway will help you choose the best way forward for formally ending your relationship. Some of the strengths and weaknesses of this option may surprise you.

This chapter offers you opportunities to understand:

- the big picture of lawyer-assisted negotiation in the separation process
- the advantages and disadvantages of lawyer-assisted-negotiation
- the importance of staying in control of your separation process

Lawyer-assisted (lawyer-to-lawyer) negotiation

This type of lawyer-assisted negotiation is typically used in situations where:

- conflict is present and a resolution is not achievable otherwise
- intense power imbalances are present between the parties
- there is a preference for remote communication
- there is enough information about the property pool and issues disputed to enable your lawyer to negotiate and represent you effectively

For whatever reason, not everyone is a fan of communicating directly with their former partner.

Be sure that you do not simply hand over control of your matter to your family lawyer if this is the pathway you choose. Stay in control of the communication made on your behalf. Make it very clear to your lawyer that all correspondence to your Ex is to be approved by you first. If you do not do this, you run the risk of having your Ex react negatively to the letter drafted on your behalf.

Regrettably (and this comes from an abundance of anecdotal evidence from family law clients and family lawyers themselves), it is all too common for lawyers to write aggressive, hurtful letters which disregard the multiple harmful impacts. They can cause personal psychological injury to the party receiving the letter (you or your Ex); inflame antipathy between you and your Ex; protract resolution of the matter; and cost you more money in legal fees. Offensive letters are unprofessional and a sign of bad lawyering. Such letters are about the other lawyer who is clearly disregarding the obligation to progress the matter to a close with outcomes which help both parties get on with their lives.

Make clear to your lawyer that you require the tone of correspondence exchanged between lawyers to be firm but civil, respectful and professional. Instruct your lawyer that you find offensive letters unacceptable and for your lawyer to make this clear to the lawyer representing your Ex.

Be sure to make it clear to your lawyer that you are not prepared to waste time or money on protracted bargaining or tolerate obstruction by your Ex. Instruct your lawyer to also make this clear to the lawyer representing your Ex. Further, in each correspondence drafted by your family lawyer for you to approve, ensure that your lawyer clearly indicates a reasonable time period for a response from the other party, say, ten working days.

How might you go about making these important points clear to your lawyer? Why not consider the following script?

> ***You:*** *The issue of correspondence between you and the other lawyer is one that is important to me and I want to make sure you understand this.*
>
> ***Lawyer:*** *Sure. I'm listening.*

***You:** I do not want any unpleasantness or aggressive language from you to my Ex's lawyer. I know _______ will only dig his heels in if he gets a letter with combative language. I know this man. I was married to him for thirty years.*

***Lawyer:** I assure you, _______, I will be careful with my correspondence.*

***You:** If you do not take care with your language this whole process could end in disaster, and I am determined to avoid this. I want things to go as smoothly as possible. This means that I want the letter you write to his lawyer to be firm and clear but not hostile.*

***Lawyer:** For the record, I am not in the habit of writing letters that are not constructive to the process.*

***You:** I would appreciate it if you would make it clear to the other lawyer that I will not tolerate aggressive or hurtful letters.*

***Lawyer:** I have to admit that I have received some letters that do not help the negotiation between separating couples. I find that disappointing and unprofessional.*

***You:** Also, can you make it clear that I have no intention of putting up with delays or any kind of silly games from _______ or his lawyer. So, I want the letters to give a deadline for a response from _______.*

***Lawyer:** I do that anyway, as a matter of practice.*

***You:** I want to approve any letters you draft before they are sent to _______'s lawyer. I want to make sure that I am involved in the progress of the case at every step of the way.*

***Lawyer:** Oh, okay. I will try to make that happen. There are times where that will not be possible. For example, if _______'s lawyer phones me about an issue. But I will let you know, in any case.*

***You:** Thank you. I appreciate that.*

Ensuring courtesy between lawyers is the most constructive, positive and inexpensive manner in which to proceed with this legal option. There are plenty of great family lawyers who have worked together as counterparts (not adversaries) who are focused solely on working effectively to get their client the best outcome.

The advantages and disadvantages of lawyer-assisted negotiation are summarised below.[61]

Assessing Lawyer-Assisted Negotiation

Advantages	Disadvantages
Your legal rights and entitlements are protected as a trained professional will be negotiating on your behalf.	The style of the negotiation may be out of your hands. An unduly aggressive negotiation style can lead to further conflict rather than resolution.
Can be cost effective where it involves lawyers who know and trust each other.	Timeframes can be difficult. You will be subject to the availability of your solicitor and, to some degree, your Ex's lawyer. This means it often will take two weeks to receive a response to correspondence so the turnaround time for negotiation by letter can be lengthy, which can quickly become very frustrating.
Removes you from the direct negotiation which can assist, particularly if there is conflict between you and your Ex.	As there is little formality to this type of negotiation, it can last a long time and sometimes can become very expensive very quickly.

Conclusion

Being informed and committed to staying in control of the process to protect your interests are essential. Be savvy. Know what can be achieved and know what your lawyer is doing and why. Future chapters will build on your interaction with your lawyer.

12
Mediation

Alternative Dispute Resolution (ADR) does not involve the adversarial process of law. ADR supports the right for separating couples to cooperatively engage with each other in dispute resolution processes that help determine their futures.[62] Mediation is a key model of ADR, just like the Collaborative Law process discussed in the following chapter. Mediation has rapidly become a popular way for separating couples in low conflict to legally complete their separation. Moreover, in Australia, participating in mediation or some alternative form of resolution is necessary to receive a Genuine Steps Certificate to prove to the Court that best endeavours have been made to settle out of Court. The purpose of this chapter is to help you understand the option of mediation.

This chapter offers you opportunities to understand:

- the big picture of mediation
- the types of mediation
- the stages of mediation
- how to prepare for mediation

Alternative dispute resolution

Mediation has become a popular choice for separating couples because it appears to be more efficient and is less expensive than going to Court (all negotiation-based options are expected to be less expensive than going to Court). Bargaining can take place in various ways: in person, by email or letter, via Skype/Zoom or telephone, and even by text message.

As I indicated at the start of this book, your choice of lawyer is crucial. If you are opting for mediation, be sure to understand that your choice of mediator is just as important.

> The skills of your chosen mediator are essential to the success of your mediation. Take the time to ensure that you have chosen an experienced mediator. Seek testimonials and input from your advisors. If your lawyer is nominating a mediator, ask them why they consider them to be the right fit for your case. A talented mediator will balance legal knowledge with personal skill. The skill is in making you and your Ex comfortable and empowered to make difficult decisions in what can be a pressured environment. A mediator is not there to give you legal advice or push you into a settlement. They may, however, reality test proposals or identify some pitfalls.[63]

The popularity of mediation has meant that the number of professionals now practising as mediators has expanded rapidly. While many mediators derive from psychology and counselling backgrounds and include talented practitioners familiar with family law, you may prefer to choose a mediator who is a lawyer experienced in mediation.

Be sure that you discuss the process with your mediator before proceeding so that you can assess whether the mediator has a sufficient sense of empathy and sensitivity to power issues between you and your former partner. If your relationship has been same-sex, gender-diverse, included mental health issues, disability issues or is culturally outside of English as a first language, then you need also to clarify that a close understanding of these issues are within the mediator's competencies.

Private mediation

A private mediation is voluntary and confidential. The mediator will likely charge a fee for two to four hours or a whole day, depending on the circumstances. You can choose the mediator (unless Court-ordered) and the type of mediation you seek. For example, in the process of *Advisory* mediation, the mediator is independent of both you and your Ex and will offer views on likely orders to be made by the Court. In this environment the mediator will identify a range of outcomes within which the Court may settle. There is a purpose to identifying this range. This range (referred to as the 'boundaries of resolution') is used to encourage the parties to the mediation to negotiate and settle within this range.

Mediation regarding children

If you are a parent of minor-aged children, it is important you understand that the Court requires a certificate from a Family Dispute Resolution Practitioner before you can make an Application for Parenting Orders.[64]

Situations which involve mediation regarding the best interests of the children can involve either Child-Inclusive or Child-Focused Mediation processes. To put it bluntly, your choice of process will likely depend on the personal maturity and conflict level of both you and your Ex.

Child-Inclusive Mediation

Child-Inclusive Mediation is an option which includes the presence of the Family Dispute Resolution Practitioner and a child expert who focus on helping parents reach a workable arrangement for the family. The children are present only at certain points of the mediation.

The defining features of Child-Inclusive Mediation are:

- consulting with children (without parents being present) in a supportive, developmentally appropriate manner about their experiences of family separation and dispute
- ensuring that the style of consultation avoids and removes any burden of decision-making from the children
- understanding and formulating children's core experience within a developmental framework
- validating children's experiences and providing basic information that may assist their present and future coping

- forming a strategic therapeutic loop back to the children's parents by considering with them the essence of their children's experience in a manner that is supportive of them hearing and reflecting upon their children's needs
- ensuring that the ongoing mediation/litigation process and the agreements or decisions that are reached reflect, at their core, the psycho-developmental needs of each child.[65]

This relies on establishing workable parenting arrangements. Screening of families takes place under this model in order to determine if the child-inclusive model is appropriate for you. If the Family Dispute Resolution Practitioner determines that the family is appropriate, parents will be required to follow a process where:

- parents are to attend joint sessions with the Family Dispute Resolution Practitioner
- Family Dispute Resolution Practitioner explains the child-inclusive model and what it involves, and answers parents' questions
- the children will be interviewed separately by a child consultant, without the parents or Family Dispute Resolution Practitioner being present
- the child consultant discusses with the children their experiences of parents' separation, current parenting arrangements, answers any questions or worries they might have, and feedback about future parenting arrangements
- the child consultant seeks information from the children regarding feedback the children want to be passed along to their parents
- the child consultant attends the parents' family dispute resolution session to discuss the feedback.[66]

The role of the child expert is to talk to you and your Ex and to the children to discover the issues that need resolving. When the child expert dedicates time to talk with your children, the expert will know that children rarely tell their parents the truth for fear of hurting their feelings or making things worse when all the children want is to make things better. Very likely they want the family back together again.

Thus, when the child consultant joins the Family Dispute Resolution Practitioner in your mediation sessions, the child consultant will provide you with feedback from talking to both you and the other parent and with feedback from talking to your children. The aim of doing this is to help you and your Ex work together to improve your arrangements for caring for the children.

This model is appropriate in situations where:

- the family has been assessed by the Family Dispute Resolution Practitioner as being appropriate for this mediation model
- the child consultant is qualified and trained to talk to children about their perspectives and feed this back to parents in a sensitive and appropriate manner
- the children are old enough to express their perspectives
- parents are able to deal with feedback in a child-focused way and are both wanting to work towards parenting arrangements that are in the best interests of the children.[67]

While it may appear the healthiest democratic option to directly involve your children in this dispute resolution process, it is important that you be aware that there are those Family Dispute Resolution Practitioners who worry that this process is not fair on the children. There are a couple of reasons for this. First, when the children provide feedback to the family consultant who then passes that feedback to parents, one or both parents may react negatively to children or outright punish them. Second, experienced Family Dispute Resolution Practitioners note that the views of the children lose significance if the case proceeds to a Court hearing.[68]

Child-Focused Mediation

Child-Focused Mediation contrasts with Child-Inclusive Mediation by the lack of direct participation of children. Children are not active participants in the process even though their best interests drive the acceptable outcomes of this type of mediation. This process directs parents' attention to the centrality of the best interests of the children throughout the mediation sessions.

You may consider it strange to distinguish between the two mediation processes because all mediation or family dispute resolution processes which involve children are essentially child-focused. What does child-focused really mean? Typically, the child-focused family dispute resolution process seeks to:

- create an environment that supports disputing parents in actively considering the unique needs of their children
- facilitate a parenting agreement that preserves significant relationships and supports children's psychological adjustment to the separation, including recovery from parental acrimony and protection from further conflict
- support parents to leave the dispute resolution forum on higher rather than diminished ground with respect to their post-separation parenting
- ensure that the ongoing mediation/litigation process and the agreements or decisions reached reflect the basic psycho-developmental needs of each child, to the extent that they can be known without the involvement of the children.[69]

The child-focused model allows the Family Dispute Resolution Practitioner to direct parents' attention to information that supports their decision-making in the best interests of the children. The Family Dispute Resolution Practitioner 'can at various stages during the mediation draw the clients' attention to information that may assist them to focus on parenting arrangements that are developmentally appropriate for their children and suited to their children's personalities and educational and extracurricular commitments'.[70]

The mediation process

There are typical stages involved in the mediation process. These stages are listed below. Remember, your choice of mediator will matter.[71]

Stages of Mediation

Pre-mediation	This stage involves an assessment of whether you and your Ex are suitable for seeking mediation (e.g. there are no power imbalances between you such as domestic violence or mental ill health) and whether the mediation process is a suitable option for your situation. This is a careful screening process. The background of the separation and questions asked determine the extent to which you and your Ex consider negotiation viable. This stage is referred to as the 'information gathering' stage and it typically occupies the majority of the mediation process.
Mediation	The mediator makes an opening statement which clarifies the process, the goals of the process, the mediator's role, the roles of each party, and the extent of confidentiality and admissibility. The mediator also clarifies that the agreement reached must be recorded in writing. In so doing, the mediator complies with the relevant legislation and is obliged to do so. At this stage, you and your Ex also make opening statements. You and your Ex then identify your goals for the mediation and the issues you are seeking to resolve. Having listened and clarified that both parties understand the issues, the mediator then works with you and your Ex to identify common issues that essentially craft the structure of the discussion. A list of issues is drawn up and referred to as the 'agenda'.
Exploration phase	The mediator follows through with the agenda, dealing with each issue, and encourages the parties to discuss the issues directly. The mediator facilitates the discussion.
Generating options	The mediator encourages you and your Ex to consider options for resolution, having discussed the issues and identified each party's interests.
Negotiation	With the assistance of the mediator, you and your Ex can pursue your respective interests by making offers and counter offers.

Resolution	At the conclusion of the mediation, you and your Ex reach an agreement on some or all of the issues on the agenda. Parties are encouraged to have the agreement formalised in writing by the mediator. If an understanding is *not* reached, then at least one positive outcome will be an understanding of each former partner's interests.
Issuing of certificate	If parenting issues are in play, and if the relevant state/country's legislation requires it, a Certificate of Mediation is issued. In Australia, a Genuine Steps Certificate will be required to prove to the Court that you have made your best efforts to come to an agreement with your Ex before filing your proposed Consent Orders.

How best to prepare for mediation

This section provides you with some practical tips for preparing for your mediation. Upon reading them, they will seem logical to you. Many people tend to forget simple issues when they are under pressure and stressed. Given its importance, thorough preparation for mediation is required.

Make lists

As with all thorough preparation, you should list the issues you want to address, goals you want to achieve, the priority of these goals, and outcomes you seek from the mediation process. This will be useful not only for thinking through the issues and ordering your thoughts, but it will be an invaluable reference in the mediation process. List all issues, both major and minor. Ensure that you list all the topics you need to address, such as outstanding debts, the house, the children, future parenting, precious items, finance, and future communication. Be specific in your list. *Be sure to include the concessions you can live with and alternatives you would be prepared to consider—what you will not move on and what you will be prepared to rethink.*

The following list is not exhaustive, so please do what works for you. List the following:

- the outcomes you want from your mediation
- your mediation issues, goals and priorities
- the topics that are especially important to you to raise in the mediation
- the major issues you want to raise in the mediation
- the minor issues you want to raise in the mediation
- the issues where you would be prepared to compromise
- the issues upon which there will be opposing viewpoints
- recurring themes of arguments with your Ex during your relationship
- any personal vulnerabilities which might undermine your success during mediation and how you will address them.

When drafting your Mediation Plan why not use the model below? Set out a large piece of paper and use your first draft to workshop your plan. Future drafts will follow until you reach the point of refining the plan to your satisfaction. You will then be confident you have covered everything and, in the process, reinforced and applied your understanding of the mediation process.

Mediation Plan

Issue	Documentation	Outcome for You	Outcome for Other	Agreement Reached

Your approach

Ask yourself questions to help identify your issues and priorities. Your lawyer will be able to assist you with this task. If your mediation were to go well, what would it look like? What outcomes would you have achieved? Having your list as a ready reference point during mediation will not only enable you to ensure all points are addressed, but it will help you manage any nervousness you may feel.

Reflect on likely opposing viewpoints

Spending some time reflecting on past arguments with your former partner will help you appreciate their perspective on issues to be discussed at mediation. Think carefully about the themes or common issues which recurred in your arguments. Consider also the behaviours demonstrated during these conflicts. These may have included:

- feelings of superiority
- feelings of irrelevance
- the insistence on being in control
- the resistance to being controlled
- feeling worthless
- fear of intimacy
- rejection of intimacy
- fear of being abandoned
- lack of trust.

When you reflect on these common issues and behaviours, you become wise as to why your Ex took the positions they did at the time and will be likely to take again during mediation. There is no guarantee that your Ex will have engaged in any critical reflection on their position in preparation for the mediation process (if they have, then bargaining will likely be easier). Your own reflections will enable you to proceed with an added strength borne of clarity.

Assemble information

Gather the relevant information for each of the topics on your list (e.g. financial statements, third party valuations or appraisals, inventories, and so on). Having the relevant documents at the ready will contribute to the efficiency of achieving an agreement. Make sure that you organise a folder to store your information and that the documents are clearly labelled so that you can easily locate them. Do not forget to bring the information to the mediation!

Do not proceed without consulting your experts

The importance of drawing on expert legal advice for your mediation cannot be overestimated. Do not commence mediation without first consulting your family lawyer. There are important legal issues in play during the settlement of your financial and parenting affairs. Your lawyer can also help you identify key issues and suggest options for achieving the results you want. And if you need to have the expertise of a financial advisor, then be sure to get the information you need to put your case forward, and for all of the issues to be addressed. Independent advice from your lawyer and financial advisor will be invaluable in reassessing your vision of your future financial security and parenting.

Questions about Mediation

For those who are not familiar with what mediation is and what it involves, many questions will likely arise. For a face-to-face or Skype or Zoom conferencing negotiation (which can be important for people with disabilities, mental illness, and those who reside in rural/remote locations), it would be worth asking a family lawyer questions which may include the following:

- What will be expected of you?
- What do pre-mediation conferences involve?
- What might the process look like on the day/s?
- To whom do I need to talk?

- How much does it cost?
- Will my Ex and I share the costs of mediation?
- Can I take breaks during the session?
- What if my Ex tries to manipulate or pressure me?
- To what extent am I expected to compromise?
- What happens if we cannot reach agreement?
- Does the principle of 'without prejudice' apply in mediation if it should break down?
- Will the Court accept my Genuine Steps Certificate if my Ex refuses to cooperate or we fail to reach an agreement?
- How much risk is there that we will not arrive at agreements?
- Will my case require more than one mediation session to achieve settlement?
- How much authority does the mediator have?
- Is the agreement legally binding?

These questions need thorough answers which can be provided by your family lawyer in your individual case.

Organise your diary to include the day and follow up sessions

Patience is required for mediation. There is no advantage to rushing through issues. If you need to follow up your initial mediation session with other sessions, then accept the necessity for progressing carefully through the mediation process. Make sure you clear your diary before and after each scheduled mediation session so that you are totally focused on the demands of the mediation process that day. Ensure that you can devote undivided attention to each of the tasks you have to perform to complete the process, including preparation. In scheduling your day, think ahead and remove competing considerations so that you are not distracted in any way.

Resist pressure and do not pressure

Mediation is an emotional and tiring process. Small tasks can drain your energy. You may be nervous, anxious, afraid of escalating conflict, or angry, resentful, uncooperative, aggressive, and so on. Do not allow your emotions to impair your decision-making. There are simply too many negative consequences which result from poor decisions, inexperience in thinking on your feet, overcompensating, compliance, destructive resistance, aggression, and failure to understand the mediation process. Do not feel compelled to make decisions then and there. Decisions can be postponed until the next mediation session. It is essential that your preparation for your mediation include your decisions about what item and issues you will be willing to give leeway since this is a major bump in the road for many people.

Prepare yourself emotionally, mentally and physically

Give yourself plenty of time to prepare and focus on the issues and process. Make sure you are rested and have eaten. Do not be afraid to take rest breaks from mediation so that you can manage your stress, eat a snack and hydrate. All of these things will help you maintain energy and concentration.

Conclusion

All of the options identified in this book require careful thought and discussion with a family lawyer. Fundamental to such careful thought is the use of questions. There is no such thing as a 'dumb question'. Your separation process is too important to worry about embarrassment. Ask and ask again. Ask until you understand. Then proceed with purpose.

Directory of Mediation Practitioners in Australia, New Zealand, United Kingdom, Canada and United States of America

Australia	
Family Dispute Resolution Providers	fdrr.ag.gov.au
Australian Mediation Association	ama.asn.au
New Zealand	
Arbitrators and Mediators Institute of New Zealand	aminz.org.nz
United Kingdom	
Family Mediation Council	familymediationcouncil.org.uk
Canada	
Canadian Mediation Association	canadianmediationassociation.ca
United States	
American Bar Association	americanbar.org (general)

13
The collaborative law process

The purpose of this chapter is to provide you with an understanding of the collaborative law process as an option for completing your relationship separation. Like mediation, the collaborative law process has its origins in the ADR movement, which grew out of a strong dissatisfaction with the perceived harmful outcomes of traditional adversarial approaches.

This chapter offers you opportunities to understand:

- what the collaborative law process involves
- how to prepare for the collaborative law process
- the advantages and disadvantages of the collaborative law process option

What the collaborative law process involves

One of the more cooperative options available to you for the legal process of ending your relationship is the collaborative law process. The appeal of this approach is that it typically does not involve spending excessive amounts of money, it does not escalate the psychological damage on everyone concerned, and it avoids protracted conflict. However, like all options, it is not without its problems.

This chapter takes a brief look at what the collaborative law process involves, as well as an overview of its advantages and disadvantages. Should you reside in Australia, New Zealand, Canada, the United Kingdom or the United States, the option of the collaborative law process is similar.

Let's get something straight from the start. The collaborative law process is *not* a soft option. There are several reasons why this process is not for everyone. ADR does not mean less accountability than adversarial approaches. If you are someone who sees the collaborative law process as the easiest method to get your own way, then the collaborative law process is *not* for you. If you are someone who is seeking revenge or hiding financial information, then this process is most certainly *not* for you. For others, such a face-to-face approach is too direct and personally confronting. They prefer the distance, time and space to reflect that the process of lawyer-assisted negotiation allows.

If working together to achieve mutually agreeable outcomes has some appeal for you and you are genuine about working with your Ex to achieve such outcomes, the collaborative law process may be the best pathway for you.

What the Collaborative Law process involves

The collaborative law process involves you and your lawyer working collaboratively with your former partner and their lawyer to identify the key issues of concern. Through exchanging points of view and expressing priorities, you and your Ex ideally arrive at an agreed outcome. Collaborative law is usually conducted through a series of 'four-way' face-to-face meetings.

When required, other experts such as financial advisors, accountants, psychologists, and/or support personnel can be involved to assist you in your decision-making. You can expect the process to involve meetings which last for two to three hours. Typically, the number of meetings to complete the process ranges anywhere from two to seven meetings, depending on the level of complexity of issues. While the goal of the collaborative law process is a legally binding settlement, it would be a mistake to think that the collaborative law process is without tension.

Let's take a look at the key rules of the collaborative law process.

Rules with which to comply

Screening for intake (eligibility) is necessary to ensure that both parties are safe, that there is not a power imbalance, and that personality disorders are not present. Unlike mediation, there are some rules of which you must be aware when considering the collaborative law process. These rules apply in all collaborative law processes no matter what state or country you live in.

- At the outset of the process both parties must sign a Participation Agreement to commit themselves to the collaborative law process.
- Signing this commitment also entails an agreement not to litigate or threaten to litigate.
- Should either you or your former partner threaten or express an intention to litigate, the process collapses.
- Parties and their lawyers attend a series of what have been termed 'four-way' face-to-face meetings, in which negotiations take place.
- The parties and their lawyers use interest-based negotiation to focus discussions on the interests of both parties.
- If agreement cannot be reached and litigation appears to be the only viable option, then lawyers representing the parties will withdraw from the process.[72]

ADR does not always mean less expense. Collaborative law can be, at times, an expensive process. Collaborative law meetings can be complex and involve experts other than your lawyer. Their fees will need to be paid on top on the fees charged by your lawyer.

Deciding whether the collaborative law process is the right way to proceed with your separation requires you to genuinely take stock of your values, your personality and your current relationship with your former partner. The following exercise will help you further clarify whether the collaborative law process is for you. After you have completed this exercise for yourself, try answering the statements from your Ex's perspective. After all, this is a process that requires planning.

How do you know if the collaborative law process is right for you?

It is worth considering the following propositions to gauge how you react to each one. Feel free to tick the propositions which resonate with you.

- ☐ I genuinely accept that the relationship is over and that the purpose of the process is to finalise arrangements so that we can each move on with our life.
- ☐ I am fully committed to preparing for the process and being able to express my needs, goals and priorities while considering those of my Ex.
- ☐ I am prepared to resolve the issues rather than focus on blaming my Ex.
- ☐ I genuinely, absolutely, want to control my own behaviour and not the behaviour of my Ex in this process.
- ☐ I am prepared to communicate respectfully with my Ex, even though we may disagree on important issues.
- ☐ I am fully committed to attending each session in the collaborative law process and prepared to participate effectively.
- ☐ I am prepared to listen to the guidance of the collaborative law professionals involved and listen to points of view other than my own.
- ☐ I genuinely appreciate that the views of my Ex are just as important as my own.
- ☐ I genuinely appreciate that my Ex has needs which deserve my respectful consideration.
- ☐ I am committed to respecting the best interests of our children, regardless of how I might feel about parenting arrangements.
- ☐ I am committed to working cooperatively with my Ex rather than having to win at all costs.
- ☐ I am committed to achieving solutions rather than resorting to combat and court proceedings.
- ☐ I am committed to honouring the terms of the agreement we will finally reach.

Did you answer 'yes' to any of these propositions?

If you honestly answered 'yes' to these questions, then the collaborative law process might be the right process for you. Did you go through the propositions from your Ex's perspective? Do you think that your Ex would respond well to the propositions? Are you both in a position where you can discuss this option with each other honestly? You would be well advised to discuss this issue at length with your Ex since preparation will be necessary.

Preparation will determine how effectively you participate

If you find that there are certain contentious issues between you and your Ex that might imperil a cooperative process, then discuss this with your family lawyer. Your success in the collaborative law process will be helped by your assessment of the contentious issues between you and your Ex.

If communication is a problem (as it is frequently in relationship breakdowns), then this needs to be addressed since the need for clear and open communication in the collaborative law process is without doubt. If either you or your Ex needs to consult a psychologist for one or two sessions, allow time for this so the process has the best chance of remaining constructive and cooperative.

Disqualification from the process

The collaborative law process has firm rules regarding issues and actions which can disqualify you or your Ex from proceeding with the collaborative law process.

Safety is a paramount issue as well as the integrity of the process, whereby you and your Ex can fully participate in the process without intimidation or restriction. The potentially disqualifying issues include (but are not limited to):

- a history of domestic violence and/or abuse perpetrated by you or your Ex
- if you or your Ex suffer from mental illness that restricts participation in the process
- the presence of a medical condition, e.g. dementia, which restricts either you or your Ex from understanding and engaging with the process
- if you or your Ex engage in chemical or substance abuse
- the presentation of pronounced anger either by you or your Ex.

It is the responsibility of the collaborative law process lawyers to carefully screen parties who elect to proceed with the collaborative law process. The lawyers acting for you and your Ex have guidelines which must be followed to ensure that the process has integrity and that all issues are addressed, communication is open and respectful, and that matters are resolved fairly and in compliance with the governing legislation.

Only *you* can know whether the option of the collaborative law process is right for you. Making sure that you understand what the collaborative law process involves is part of this decision-making process. It is important that you understand the limitations of the collaborative law process as well as its purported strengths. There is one fact of which you can be sure: *your choice of lawyer will always be the key factor in whatever process you choose.*

Your deliberations will include an assessment of advantages and disadvantages of the collaborative law process. It is therefore advisable to consider each.

Advantages of the collaborative law process

Exponents of collaborative law pronounce its benefits as follows:

- It is a civilised, non-adversarial approach in which ex-partners work together with the assistance of their lawyers to achieve their goals.
- It is less stressful than working adversarially. It's a much less stressful way to determine the decisions and outcomes between you and your former partner.

- It allows flexibility.
- It can be a process tailored to reflect the needs of the parties concerned.
- It can generate a range of alternatives and creative solutions.
- It is family-oriented to arrive at outcomes that are positive for the whole family.
- It is focused on problem-solving.
- It is settlement-focused, guided by both parties' goals and interests.
- It fosters a holistic approach by allowing the involvement of experts such as child experts, financial advisors, accountants, psychologists, and personal support advisors.
- It is often far cheaper than a negotiated (lawyer correspondence) settlement or going to court.
- The process allows you to maintain your self-respect.[73]

Disadvantages of the collaborative law process

Concerns anecdotally expressed by some lawyers and clients when reflecting on their collaborative law experience have included the following:

- The pressure on lawyers to perform in front of the other lawyer and get results in front of their clients may interfere with the integrity of the collaborative approach.
- It can be very expensive if, at some point during one of the collaborative law sessions, one of the parties gives up and indicates that they want a different process or wants to go to court. This means that both lawyers are compelled to withdraw and the settlement process has to start over from scratch. And this means lots more legal fees.
- There can be a disparity in the skill levels between lawyers, e.g. one collaborative law trained lawyer is less experienced and/or one lawyer has sharper negotiating skills.
- There may be pressure on the parties to sign at the conclusion of the collaborative law process rather than allowing the parties to go away

and reflect on what has been agreed on and what has emerged from the process.

- Women in heterosexual separation situations are more likely to be psychosocially disadvantaged given pre-existing power relationships (which do not invite disqualification).
- Differences in power dynamics may exist for all relationships, including same-sex, gender-diverse and mixed culture separations.
- Lawyers may not be across key issues for clients with a disability, same-sex relationships, or mixed culture separations.
- There may be pressure on each of the parties by advisors to concede aspects of property division and clients are not assertive enough to decline such advice from their only ally in the room.
- The level of training practitioners undertake can vary. Beginner training courses tend to run for two to three days. Advanced training has recently become available in some states/countries.[74]

Of course, these observations by lawyers and clients may be particular to the situations in which they were working. Your context may be different, but it is wise to be aware of the views of others.

How can you prepare for the collaborative law process?

Here are some suggestions for how to best prepare for the collaborative law process:

- Discuss beforehand with your collaborative lawyer your understanding of the collaborative law process and your concerns about communicating with your Ex and their lawyer.
- Document your interests, priorities and concessions you would be prepared to make.
- Reality-check your interests and priorities.

- Develop your understanding of interest-based negotiation and basic negotiation skills.
- Rehearse what you want to say and rehearse again and again.
- Research views expressed by exponents and opponents of the collaborative law approach.

Conclusion

If you and your Ex can cooperate, then you will qualify for the collaborative law process. Self-awareness is essential in choosing the legal option for your separation. Understanding what is involved in the option you choose and thinking through the consequences of your decisions will remain important throughout the process.

Whatever your separation journey involves, stay focused.

Directory of Collaborative Law Practitioners

Australia	
Melbourne Collaborative Alliance	melca.com.au
Collaborative Professionals NSW	collabprofessionalsnsw.org.au
Queensland Collaborative Law	qcl.org.au
Collaborative Practice SA	collaborativepracticesa.com.au
Collaborative Professionals WA	collaborativeprofessionalswa.com.au
Collaborative Alliance Tasmania	collaborativealliancetas.com
International	
International Academy of Collaborative Professionals	collaborativepractice.com

14
Parenting plans

In 2020, there were 7.2 million families in Australia. 1 million (14.2%) were one parent families with 79.3% of these headed by single mothers. This reflects the formidable numbers of separated parents.[75] If you are a parent who is undertaking relationship separation, this chapter applies to you. How you handle your parenting arrangements can make a significant difference to your legal fee spend, let alone your children. The priority of this chapter is to encourage you to think decisively and plan in a realistic and productive manner that reflects the Court's principle of 'the best interests of the child'.

This chapter offers you opportunities to understand:

- the basics of the paramountcy principle, 'the best interests of the child'
- the considerations that can be in your parenting plan
- the different issues which matter to your parenting arrangements

Parenting

As a thoughtful parent, only *you* know what is best for you and what steps need to be taken for your situation. Trust yourself. You *know* that your children need routine and caring. When the Court insists that the principle of 'the best interests of the child' be respected, you had better believe the Court means it. You *know* that you need to remain involved in your children's activities and care-giving, and to avoid bad-mouthing the other parent. You *know* that it is a bad look if you deny your former partner access to the children if there is no abuse present, and the children are happy to spend time with the other parent. And you *know* to ensure that you communicate clearly with your children so that *they* know what is happening and why.

What does 'the best interests of the child' mean?

The term 'family dispute resolution' is used to refer to mediation, one of the purposes of which is to discuss parenting arrangements. For instance, in Australia, it is compulsory for parents to undertake family dispute resolution before being permitted to initiate proceedings.

Attending (compulsory) mediation with a Court-registered Family Dispute Resolution Practitioner will contribute to convincing the Court that you are both committed to the responsible care of your children. The Court is guided by the paramountcy principle of 'the best interests of the child' of which there are two aspects.[76] These two aspects serve also to remind parents that the *children* have rights in the situation of parental separation. The interests of the children take precedence over the individual interests of the parents.

The first aspect to the paramountcy principle of the 'best interests of the child' is that children have the right to receive adequate and proper parenting to help them reach their full potential. The second aspect is that parents must fulfil their obligations to provide care, welfare and development for their children.[77] Such a commitment to responsible care is typically expressed in a formal document known as a Parenting Plan or Parenting Order by Consent. Such a plan, in some states/countries, does not need to be registered with the Court. Check this fact with your lawyer/attorney if you live outside of Australia.

Another important issue to note is the change in attitudes towards a more inclusive, insightful society. As we learn more about same-sex relationships, the law (in some countries) has been adjusted regarding sexual orientation and parenting. The 2016 Australian Census reported that 15% of Australian families were same-sex parents. The Census reported that 4.5% of self-identified gay men and 25% of self-identified lesbians have children.[78] In this area, it will be rewarding to see advances in law reform and Court approaches to same-sex parents and their children.

The prospect of collaborating with the other parent in aid of the children will be, for some parents, daunting. Too often children are used as pawns to leverage a favourable property settlement. Battle lines are drawn and toxicity threatens to be financially ruinous for both parents. Understand that the Court takes a dim view of parents who refuse to act in the interests of the children, or participate at all. Custody battles which end up in Court are simply ugly. Ugly, expensive and worst of all, damaging to children. It only takes one parent to make life for children a nightmare.

Parenting plans

Developing a Parenting Plan requires a lot of careful thinking. Co-operation between you and your Ex can result in a Parenting Plan that works best for your children in the first instance, and both parents in the second. A Parenting Agreement based on co-operation and reviewed by a lawyer typically does not need to be filed in Court. A Parenting Plan is a 'living document' which means that when the needs of your children change (especially when the children are young or the situation of the parents changes) both you and your Ex can agree in writing to update the Plan. You are best advised to formalise your updated Parenting Plan. For parents who cooperate to make the best possible Parenting Plan for the children, this can be a relatively straightforward process.

While a Parenting Plan does not have to be filed, registered in Court, or issued as a formal Court Order, there are legal requirements which apply in order to make the Plan legally valid. The Parenting Plan must be:

- in writing
- signed and dated by both you and the other parent
- relevant to the children's living arrangements, contact with each parent, health and wellbeing (see the Parenting Plan template at the end of this chapter)
- made free of duress, threats or coercion.[79]

You need to be flexible with the arrangements that are drafted into a Parenting Plan. This helps prevent misunderstandings down the track. For instance, when parents re-partner or other changes occur, if you have issues that need discussion between parents, a Parenting Plan protects the best interests of your children. It is crucial that you understand the most important issues regarding your children in the Parenting Plan. When drafting a Parenting Plan, it is up to you to decide the order for addressing issues and to include short and long-term considerations. Perhaps you may prefer to begin with the most straightforward issues and graduate to more complex issues.

Your Parenting Plan must make very clear to the Court that you are committed to arrangements that clearly serve 'the best interests of the child'. This might be a Co-Parenting Plan, which involves (low conflict) collaboration between parents. Or it might be a Parallel Parenting Plan that allows for parenting separately, since high conflict is present between the parents.

Parents who obstruct the process will surrender important contributions to their children's wellbeing. Sabotaging the process of making arrangements for the care of your children contributes to racking up fees and simply means you will have fewer resources for your future. The best idea is to include your Parenting Plan in your proposed Consent Orders.

The mediation session with the Family Dispute Resolution Practitioner will offer you the opportunity to discover more about the mediation process.[80] The Family Dispute Resolution Practitioner will fully consider your concerns and preferences. If you do not feel safe with the other parent being in the same room, the Family Dispute Resolution Practitioner can arrange for separate locations or separate rooms in the same location.

After you have made Parenting Plan decisions, confirmed with the other parent, and have both signed off on the Plan, liaise with your children's school (you will recall I mentioned this as part of separation preparation). Make a point of talking to each of your children's classroom teachers so the teachers and the school can be an important source of support for your children. Teachers are trained to identify children who are having adjustment problems, and they can work with you to keep an eye on the situation and problem-solve with you. Many schools have counsellors, who may also be a useful resource for you.

You will find a Parenting Plan template at the end of this chapter that will help you identify, clarify and carefully plan the arrangements for parenting your children so that your children's wellbeing is protected and your responsibilities will be satisfied. Please feel free to use it.

Parallel parenting

You will no doubt realise that the major difference between co-parenting and parallel parenting is that co-parenting will involve flexibility, co-operation and on-going communication between the parents while parallel parenting does not. Parallel parenting emerges from the situations of high conflict separation.

The reasons why two parents have gone down the path of parallel parenting are important factors which shape your Parallel Parenting Plan. Even though Co-Parenting Plans are for people who can cooperate, some of their specific steps and communication strategies will still apply to Parallel Parenting Plans. However, there will be an emphasis on particular issues regarding decision-making. Please note that a Parallel Parenting Plan that does not reflect the best interests of the children, and that does not effectively address the health and wellbeing of the children, will not be approved by the Court. You may find the following feedback from parents who have parallel-parented helpful.

Resolving disagreements

First and foremost in your Parenting Plan, decide how disagreements about parenting issues should be resolved. For instance, do you call in a third party? Do you retain a child expert? Do you hire a mediator? Whatever you do, avoid making matters worse by taking your dispute to Court. It is expensive, destructive and the outcome will almost certainly not satisfy either parent. Draw on your lawyer for guidance.

Certainty

Ensure that you build certainty into every part of your Parallel Parenting Plan. For example, this includes arrangements for events which respect the need for only one of the parents to be present. The need for certainty also includes certainty about methods of communication. Why not keep a *Parenting Communication Diary*? (see overpage) Certainty prevents escalating hostility between the parents.

Managing time spent with your child responsibly

When creating a Parenting Plan, deciding how much time will be spent with your child can be a sensitive issue which needs careful thought. Days of the week, weeks of the year, holidays, birthdays, and so on, all need to be decided. Parenting experts can help you with this, depending on your particular situation. The ages of your children is also an important issue since developmental needs will factor into the responsibilities of each parent.

Reliability

Spending time with each parent requires arrangements for drop-off and pick-up. Depending on the existing level of hostility, it may be better if you organise a formal handover at your local Relationship Centre, regardless of whether you live in Australia, United Kingdom, New Zealand, Canada, or America. Many government funded family support agencies provide a range of services for families, including dispute resolution and child handovers. Depending on the situation, you may even opt to have a reliable mutual friend perform these tasks for you both. Remember, keep to the time agreed. Whatever you do, keep certainty and reliability in mind.

Timing

Timing is everything. Dependability and reliability are essential to the emotional security of your children. To make sure that your children remain emotionally secure, both parents must respect timing. Childhood trauma which resonates in adulthood can arise simply due to ugly scenes between parents due to one parent's insensitivity to punctuality. In a Parallel Parenting Plan, timing is essential and subject to the parental satisfaction of your legal obligations to responsibly care for your children. While things have not worked out between you both as partners, place your children front and centre when resolving issues.

Parenting Communication Diary

Keeping a diary which notes down all interactions between you and your Ex, and interactions between your children and your Ex, is important. Moreover, a parenting diary may be useful down the track if the other parent becomes unreliable. Be sure to note all communications such as phone calls, texts and emails (provide copies if you can). Also, try to record appointments and commitments that have been missed. Any difficulties should be noted with date, time and detail. The more detail, the better. Be sure to be reasonable and balanced in your information-recording and vigilance. Remember though, if you are in a high conflict situation, then these notations will assume greater importance.

Conclusion

As you can now appreciate, there are many issues to be considered and then factored into your Parenting Plan. Do not forget that all Parenting Plans are 'living documents'. They are documents which need to be driven by an attitude of flexibility. Why? Because the needs of children change as they develop. Children may develop ill health, have special needs or experience misadventures. Moreover, the life circumstances of parents can change, whether through new employment, death, re-partnering, impoverishment, ill health, etc. Parenting Plans can be the greatest opportunity for co-operation between parents and significant others to achieve wonderful, enriching outcomes for your children. Do not let this opportunity pass you by.

Parenting Plan Draft

These questions will help you draft a Parenting Plan. You will find these questions not only helpful in thinking through some serious issues relevant to your quality parenting but helpful in providing a starting point for working with your lawyer to negotiate the parenting arrangements that are in the best interest of your children. Remember, your responses to these questions are not based on what *you* want but the needs of your children.

1. How will decisions regarding parenting arrangements be made?
2. How will disagreements about parenting issues not addressed in the Parenting Plan be resolved?
3. What method/s will be used to resolve differences quickly so they do not impact negatively on the children?
4. Consider how you might appoint a parenting coordinator to assist you with parenting conflicts and what decision-making authority you give them.
5. What organisation to date have you made regarding your children's living and care arrangements?
6. What arrangements for the children's wellbeing will be made in the event of one of the parents dying? (e.g. update will, appointment of guardians, update insurances)
7. Where will your children live permanently?
8. Will there be a detailed schedule for pick-up and drop-off? (Consider a 'family calendar' if appropriate.)
9. What clothing, and so on, is required for changeover? (Consider two sets of clothing, if financially viable, to avoid missing items, and make changeover more streamlined and less complicated.)

10. How much time will the children spend with each parent? How often should these arrangements be reviewed?
11. Will both parents have a list of emergency telephone numbers?
12. What arrangements are to be made in the event of an emergency? Such as, if one parent has to be hospitalised, becomes disabled, incarcerated, unemployed and/or unable to contribute financially to the welfare of the children?
13. How will communication between parents and children take place when the children are not in the care of the other parent?
14. What arrangements will be made regarding the financial support of your children?
15. What arrangements will be made to address the health/medical issues of your children?
16. List details of your children's Medicare/Social Security number, health fund number, copies of medical records, details of vaccinations, allergies and illnesses the children have had.
17. Which schools/childcare facilities will your children attend?
18. How will the parents address school reports, homework, appointments with education specialists, special needs, permission slips, sick notes, bullying issues, and so on?
19. How and what decisions will be made regarding who the children spend time with and communicate with (other than the parents)?
20. Will the children have sleepovers, and who with? Which friends are the children allowed to spend social and recreational time with? Will the parents of your children's friends be aware of relevant Parenting Plan issues?

21. Are there particular people the parent regards as a threat to the welfare of the children? What arrangement will be made to protect the children?
22. Will the children spend time with grandparents? Other relatives? How much time and when? Will these people be made aware of relevant Parenting Plan issues?
23. What contact will the children have with new partners of the parents? What are these new partners to be called by your children? What should be the nature of the contact between new partners and children?
24. With whom will your children travel as passengers and what arrangements will be made for appropriate child safety seating?
25. Which values are important to you and how will they be fostered in the raising of the children? Such as, interaction with others, care of animals, education, life priorities, etc.
26. Which religious or cultural practices (if relevant) do you adhere to and how will you address them in your children's life?
27. How will those with parental responsibility communicate with each other?
28. What are the diet, sleeping and clothing arrangements for the children when staying with the other parent?
29. What financial arrangements will be made for the costs of:
    - health care, doctors, dentists, optometrists, specialists
    - insurance
    - school uniforms, books, equipment, computers and related equipment, excursions, shoes, lunches, after school care, holiday care

- sports clothes, sports equipment, travel to sporting activities
- other sports costs
- clothing for the children, laundry, return of clothes
- swimming costumes, sun cream, protective clothing and equipment, pool membership
- toiletries
- pocket money
- transport
- birthday presents
- recreation and social requirements, e.g. games, movies, events and other outings.

15
Custody of your family pet

People's family and social lives frequently revolve around their commitments to their pets. I know mine used to. The financial and emotional investment in animal members of the family is deep. The first purpose of this chapter is to alert you to the expense of custody battles over animal members of your family if post-separation caring arrangements are not managed properly. The second purpose is to establish that these arrangements should continue for the lifetime of your family pet and beyond the sad day when they pass away. These two issues are discussed against the background of the legal position of your family pet regarding your separation settlement. Many of you will likely encounter some confronting realities when it comes to the position of your family pet in family law.

This chapter offers you opportunities to understand:

- the big picture of pets in families
- the place of family pets in family law
- how to plan for the care of your family pet/s

The 'best interests' of your family pet

The 'best interests of your pet' test, which I recommend, draws on the family law principle of 'the best interests of the child' discussed in the previous chapter. To apply this principle to your family pet is to have two primary considerations. The first is to protect your family pet from harm and ensure they are well cared for. The second is to allow your family pet to have meaningful relationships with both guardians. At the end of this chapter, you will find a Pet Guardianship Plan template to help you make the decisions that are in the best interests of your pet's wellbeing.

Your family pet is important everywhere

It is commonplace for companion animals to be loved as a family member. For instance, the highly respected Australian animal welfare organisation, the Royal Society for the Prevention of Cruelty to Animals (RSPCA) reports that, 'Australia has one of the highest rates of pet ownership in the world. About 62% of Australian households own pets.[81] There are an estimated more than 24 million pets in Australia.' United States data is similar: 68% of US households, or about 85 million families, own a pet, according to the 2017–2018 National Pet Owners Survey conducted by the American Pet Products Association (APPA).[82]

Government and Census data includes population movement, activities, and productivity. People are increasingly including one or more animals in their family home and spending a substantial part of their grocery bill on food, making sure their pet is healthy by visits to the vet, going the extra mile should their pet have special needs, and taking out pet insurance. While people are engaging in activities to love and care for their animals whom they consider family members, governments are measuring the consumer spending of such activities.[83] The status of companion animals and its relevance to family law in many countries awaits recognition.

Understanding the place of your family pet

Many people consider their pets to be their children. You have very much the same bond; you love and cherish them, you spend large amounts of your time with them, you nurture and care for them, you place their sustenance as high priorities in your supermarket shopping, you think fondly about them several times a day when you are not with them, you take photographs of them and lovingly frame and place them in special locations in your home, you organise play friends for them, you protect them from harm, and even centre your recreational activities around them. And you tend your pet's graves after the devastating event of their death.

Your love for your pets is intense and represents a relationship that is supremely important in your life. The love for your pets is often part of the special bond you have with your partner. Come time for separation from your partner, the issue of who becomes primary carer for your pet can become an intensely sensitive issue. Despite the emotional and psychological significance of your pet to your family, family law in most states/countries regard animals as personal property—as possessions belonging to people—to be part of your property division upon separation.

Custody disputes

The number of separating couples who seek legal advice to fight for custody of their pet when their relationship breaks down has been rapidly increasing for more than a decade in the UK, US, and Australia.[84] Mainstream media has featured celebrity disputes over their pets, disputes which have cost excessive legal fees. Such legal battles are a common feature in the case profile of family lawyers.

The increasing number of pet custody disputes among non-celebrities in lawyer client profiles have demonstrated the expensive lengths to which separated couples will go to keep their pet with them. While some measures can be taken to ensure custody, these measures need to be approached as you would for an asset such as property. Any caring acts beyond your legal duty of care owed to animals that is enshrined in animal welfare laws, are matters of morality and judgement.

If negotiating with your Ex about custody arrangements for your pet is not an option then you do have other recourses available to you. You can seek proposed Consent Orders which include provisions for your pet or you can be explicit in your property documentation by taking 'ownership' of your pet given the current status of animals as property. Remember, a Consent

Order is a way to make agreements official after a relationship separation. It is a Court Order, but rather than going to Court and having a judge determine the fairest and most equitable option, a proposed Consent Order is made when the parties have worked out a solution between themselves. If two people can decide on arrangements for pet custody, they can then apply for proposed Consent Orders to formalise it. Nevertheless, as the numbers of pet guardians continue to rise rapidly around the world, the issue of pet custody features increasingly in the family law dispute landscape as a considerably expensive contest. Try to make sure that your case is not one of them.

Make arrangements

Making arrangements that are in the best interests of your family pet should rightly assume importance in your decision-making—just as parents of children should develop a sensible Parenting Plan. Your role as your pet's guardian is a responsible one. Responsible decision-making is the key to caring for the animal in your life. Consult a lawyer to help you if you need to.

This includes finding a family lawyer who is:

- familiar with animal law
- who is sensitive to animal issues such as the impact of conflict on them, their safety, wellbeing and care
- who understands the importance of family companion animals to you
- who is resourceful in drawing up a formal agreement akin to a Parenting Plan so that you and your Ex can both act in the best interests of your special family member.

Planning

Do not for a moment think that your pet will *not* be affected by your separation. Research confirms that separation affects pets as much as it does children. Dogs, especially, are sensitive to the loss of a guardian—*their* family member—and are very sensitive to the discord and verbal conflict that typically precedes a relationship breakdown.

> Whilst some dogs love living in two households, co-parenting isn't usually a pleasant experience for your canine companion. Indeed, switching between two worlds can be extremely confusing. So, try to stay on good terms with your ex-partner and make sure that you carefully coordinate the dog's upbringing, rules and daily routine. A new home environment can be uncomfortable for your dog, particularly if a new partner is present. A dog may also be more attached to one of the two separating partners. A dog who misses their 'favourite' owner may become depressed, which can manifest in excessive licking/scratching, peeing or pooing in the home, loss of appetite and other problem behaviours.
>
> Help your dog through this difficult period. Don't punish them if they exhibit 'naughty', disobedient or stressed behaviour. Instead, give them the time they need. After all, your dog is simply having a normal reaction to an abnormal situation. Make sure that drop-off and collection times are calm and argument-free and give your dog plenty of reassurance. Allow your dog to gradually adjust to their new life by ensuring that the new home contains familiar elements, such as their own basket and cuddly toys. And give your dog additional attention by going for long walks and showering it with affection.
>
> Cats are typically more attached to their surroundings than people, thus access arrangements tend not to be an option. A change of home will cause your cat a significant amount of stress. They may start marking their territory, try to escape or even run away. The best solution for cats and also for many dogs (and one that's increasingly common for children), is for the pet to remain in the original 'parental' home, whilst the separating partners take it in turns to stay there. This creates a stable home environment for all concerned.[85]

Animal cruelty is linked to domestic violence and child abuse. Animals are especially at risk in high conflict homes.

In Victoria, Safe Steps Family Violence Response Centre CEO, Annette Gillespie, reports that of the 90,000 calls the centre receives each year, callers express concern about the safety of animals in these high conflict situations and 40% of these family pets are already injured. The number of pets who have been killed by their abusive partners is shocking.[86] As a result, they started a Pets at Risk Program funded by Australia's Victorian Government. Pets at Risk finds homes for the animals of victims of domestic violence. In 2020, the New South Wales Government recognised that pets are hurt and killed as acts of intimidation in domestic violence situations and listed pets in their provisions for Apprehended Domestic Violence Orders.[87]

To find help with pets if you are a victim of domestic violence and need to place your pet in temporary care, consider contacting one of the following agencies:

Agencies for Animal Crisis Care in Australia

Victoria	Animal Aid Pets in Peril	(03) 9739 0300
New South Wales	RSPCA Safe Bed	(02) 9782 4408
Queensland	RSPCA Pets in Crisis	1800 811 811
Western Australia	Shelter WA	(08) 9300 0340
Northern Territory	Dawn House	(08) 8945 1388
South Australia	RSPCA Safe Kennels DV Project	1300 477 722
Tasmania	Shelter Tasmania	1800 800 588

Those of you who have left relationships and relinquished custody of your pet will know the anguish involved. If separations are not amicable, then the inability to stay in contact with the companion you came to love as intensely as you would a child can invite considerable grief. The decision to do what is best for your pet is more important than selfishly wanting your pet to stay with you because you would miss them and because you want to be the primary caregiver.

Destructive fighting over the custody of your pet does not reflect mature consideration for what is best for the animal concerned. Of course, family pets become distressed when exposed to arguments and conflict between partners who have cared for them. It is obviously not in their interest to be exposed to heated quarrels. Like children, they need a loving, caring and safe environment in which their needs are met by a trusted, responsible, animal-centred, loving guardian—someone who behaves and makes decisions in *their* best interests.

Conclusion

If the answers to the questions in the following exercise mean that your pet will be best off living with your former partner, then walk the talk of how much you love your pet and make the tough decision in your pet's favour. Laws in other western countries regarding animals in relationship separation matters are starting to show some promising changes. In a 2019 issue of the *American Bar Association Journal,* Linda Babcock reported on shifts in legal perceptions of pets as assets to family members and that 'States are passing laws that give judges a longer leash in divorce custody proceedings'.[88] Judges in these states/countries are now considering what is in the best interest of the pet. The Alaskan, Illinois, and Californian courts will consider points such as who mainly looks after the pet; who takes them to the vet; who usually gives the pet food and water; whether the pet is more attached to one owner; and who can best provide them with safe and comfortable shelter. Pet custody, visitation and financial support can be determined by the court in these American states. How about we encourage other states/countries to follow?

Pet Guardianship Plan Draft

The questions below will help you draft your Pet Guardianship Plan. You will find these questions helpful in thinking through some very serious issues relevant to your responsible caring and providing a starting point for working with your lawyer to negotiate the caring arrangements that are in the best interest of your family pet. Remember, your responses to these questions are not based on what *you* want but the needs of your family pet.

1. Which guardian is willing to be primary caregiver of the animal?
2. Is the animal safe with each guardian?
3. Is the environment of the guardian who has left the family home appropriate for the animal?
4. With which guardian would the animal be most happy living?
5. Which guardian has the greater bond with the animal?
6. Which guardian has invested greater time and money in caring for the animal?
7. Which guardian acted as primary caregiver of the animal?
8. Which guardian has the greater ability and capacity to provide for the animal's needs?
9. Are there practical difficulties for one of the guardians to care for the animal?
10. What are the attitudes of each guardian to the responsibilities of caring for the animal?
11. Which guardian has contributed substantially to the decision-making regarding the care for the animal?

12. Are both guardians willing to foster a close relationship between the animal and the non-custodial guardian?
13. Would the animal continue to be especially cared for if living with one guardian or the other?
14. Will the custodial guardian have proximity to the vet your animal is used to visiting?
15. Will the custodial guardian still have proximity to the same park where the animal likes to play with other animals and be able to play with the dogs in their regular playgroup?
16. Will the expenses for caring for them, feeding them, grooming them, and vet costs be shared equally?
17. What arrangements are to be made upon the death of your family pet? For example, maintaining a grave ?

16

Be consumer aware

The confusing world of the legal profession often distracts clients from recognising that they are consumers who are purchasing legal services from a lawyer, just as you would purchase any other service in the marketplace. Does this confusion resonate with you? Both you and your family lawyer have obligations during the transaction taking place. Moreover, as a client of a family lawyer, you have consumer protection measures should your lawyer fail to perform in accordance with legal professional rules and ethics. The mission of this chapter is to encourage you to know all of the costs and obligations involved in purchasing legal services for your separation. Be a consumer who is clear about the legal services you are purchasing.

This chapter offers you opportunities to understand:

- the general consumer issues of family law legal services
- ways to save money
- your obligations as a client
- how the legal profession is regulated
- how to act promptly in the case of unsatisfactory services

Issues to consider

What follows is an overview of relevant consumer issues and some suggestions for you to consider in order to be an informed, purposeful client.

Educate yourself

If there are issues you wish to know more about, consider researching these issues yourself to gain some understanding rather than automatically picking up the telephone or emailing your lawyer. Draw on the resources included on the website of your state's Law Society to research information about your consumer rights. Law Society websites have a dedicated community section and are staffed by talented, knowledgeable professionals who are only too happy to help you with your questions. Only when you cannot find the information online on your state/country's Family Court website, should you then contact your lawyer. You would be surprised how much money you can save by doing this.

Be sure to know all of the costs involved

Keep asking questions until you feel you have a full picture of the costs. You might even have questions that have occurred to you from reading other chapters in this book. Include them on your list to ask your lawyer the following:

- How much does your lawyer charge per hour?
- How much does your lawyer's paralegal cost?
- How much does photocopying cost?
- How much does your lawyer's document perusal cost?
- How much does reading and responding to your emails cost?
- How much for a brief telephone call?
- Does your lawyer charge by six-minute units or a fixed fee?

Make sure you get a copy of your lawyer's detailed fee structure. This is a list of all fees, charges and rates. Keep this information in your file of documents. Check all of these costs against your account each time you receive an invoice.

Find out about disbursements

At your first meeting with your lawyer, ask your lawyer to identify any disbursements involved. They are costs which are necessary for your lawyer to progress your matter. For example, filing fees with the Court Registrar are a key disbursement cost. Depending on the complexity of your matter disbursements can include subpoenas and expert reports.

You can ask for these disbursements to be individually identified in the Costs Agreement along with the fee. You can also check the fees on your state/country's Law Society website. Ask your lawyer whether they add an amount on top of the fees. If your lawyer tells you they are going to use a courier service, tell them that you will deliver the required documents to the appropriate agency (should your circumstances permit). Continually engage in cost-benefit assessments as part of being careful with your legal service spending. By taking these simple actions, along with other actions identified to guide you in this book, you can cumulatively save yourself a considerable sum of money.

Legal services log

Keep an updated log of your communications with your lawyer which includes details of the following:

- the content of consultations
- a record of the exact times you met with your lawyer and precise length of those consultations
- the telephone calls, the length of those calls, and the content of the calls
- copies of the emails from you that your lawyer is required to peruse
- copies of the emails sent to you by your lawyer
- copies of invoices
- the filing fees
- fees charged by your lawyer per six minute unit or per hour
- the work performed by your lawyer and by paralegals

- the number of pages photocopied and the cost of photocopying
- courier costs
- disbursements
- the lawyer's notice to you that sets out the attempts taken to come to an agreement with your Ex, the costs involved and the length of your matter.

A detailed log is essential for you to be across your legal services and the costs invoiced to you. It is part of the general requirement for you to be on the ball, organised and focused on completing *your* separation.

Photocopying

As mentioned earlier in this book, if photocopying of documents is required then try to ensure that *you* do the photocopying because your lawyer will charge you far more than the cost of doing it yourself. Why pay lawyers to photocopy documents when you can do it yourself? Photocopying documents at a public facility like a library will likely cost you a minimum amount of money. For example, in Australia, it might be 10 cents or 20 cents per page. However, lawyers can charge considerably more than this. Lawyers have been known to charge AU$1.00 or AU$1.50 per page for photocopying. You are not only paying for photocopying, you are paying for the labour to do so.

Lawyer billing alternatives

The changes taking place in the legal services market means there is a shift towards demonstrating greater attention to client preferences. This change includes flexible fee structures and providing greater client choice of service delivery. It is a shift which defines itself against the traditional time billing practices. This shift is also happening, in part, as a response to the greater numbers of clients who are taking the time to educate themselves about legal services they are seeking. During your search for an appropriate lawyer, you will be able to gain a sense of their billing practices by carefully reading lawyer websites. Alternatively, you may wish to consider talking to your lawyer about alternative billing arrangements like fixed fee, capped or value billing arrangements. Nowadays, many lawyers are prepared to offer, for instance, a fixed fee arrangement for fairly straightforward and low conflict matters. There is something to be said for being pragmatic about viewing your relationship with your lawyer as a business transaction.

Be bold and ask your lawyer at your first appointment how you can help reduce your legal fees. A responsive lawyer will welcome your assistance. Any lawyer who does not respond constructively to the question of how you can reduce your legal fees is probably not the lawyer for you.

Understand the realities of fixed fee service

You may have heard of the term 'fixed fee' billing and thought that a fixed fee is a good idea because you would know what costs you are facing. Fixed fee legal services are actually not a recent innovation. For instance, conveyancing for residential property has been available for a long time as a fixed fee. Given the general lack of trust in the legal profession, the certainty of legal fees is appealing to many people. In recent years more and more family lawyers have offered fixed fees and greater transparency in billing in order to be more competitive in the marketplace.

If this appeals to you, it is important that you understand the realities of fixed fee billing. You need to be clear about how lawyers can offer fixed fee pricing for their legal services.

Fixed fees can only be charged for specific blocks of work where the costs will be known in advance by the lawyer. Thus, complex matters and contested matters which have the potential to go awry are not dealt with in fixed fee arrangements. For instance, while you and your lawyer may work together efficiently, your Ex may prove to be highly uncooperative. Your lawyer cannot anticipate the costs deriving from your Ex's attitudes and behaviour.

However, there is a reality which clients would do well to remember. Price certainty appeal is one thing, but unfortunately many clients may fall into the trap of assuming that fixed fee arrangements are less expensive than time-based fees. Fixed fee does not mean 'cheaper'. It simply means cost certainty for select sections of your family law matter. It is important to remember that law firms have to operate on a commercial basis to be sustainable. This means that with every fee you are charged, your lawyer or their law firm needs to make a profit.

As such, fixed fee legal services are offered after your matter, or sections of your matter, are valued on the basis of resources required, administrative overheads anticipated, likely time spent completing tasks required to progress your matter, calculation of time in face-to-face consultations between you and your lawyer, phone calls to your lawyer, phone calls from your lawyer to you, emails to and from your lawyer, and so on. Fixed fee arrangements will typically be restricted to specific tasks where the law firm will not have to face risk or events that are not anticipated. The reality is, fixed fee arrangements are not entered into by lawyers unless they are profitable. It's that simple. So, while price certainty is great, it may be that a fixed fee charged by a law firm may turn out to be more expensive than other billing arrangements. Understanding the issues involved in fixed fee billing is important for the client so that you do not make uninformed, costly mistakes. As a client you can see that fixed fee billing offers wins for both you and your lawyer. Understanding your responsibility to constantly be across the charging of legal fees will be the driving purpose of your role as a client.

Costs agreement

All ongoing service costings provided by your lawyer are documented in a formal agreement referred to as a Cost Agreement or Retainer, depending on the state/country in which you reside. A costs agreement/retainer sets out terms, conditions, fees and services to be charged by your lawyer. See overpage for a summary of an Australian cost agreement. It would be a very wise move for you to read closely the costs agreement. Before starting work on your matter, your lawyer will provide you with this costs agreement/ retainer to read carefully and sign. Resist the pressure to sign it then and there at your first appointment. Take the costs agreement/retainer home with you to read and then re-read. Make a list of questions you want to ask your lawyer. Think carefully about the initial comments made to you by your lawyer. Does the costs agreement reflect what was discussed during your appointment? If not, ask for the costs agreement to be revised to accurately reflect what was said.

You should not be charged for this. Request all items be identified separately, for example, each type of legal service and individual disbursement. Clarify with your lawyer that wherever possible paralegals will not perform work that is required and charged to you at the rate by someone more senior. Request a notice of unexpected payments. Inform your lawyer that you want to be notified *before* your funds are spent on an item that you have not discussed. Also inform your lawyer that if your legal fees are going to be higher than those quoted in your costs agreement, you are to be notified as soon as possible. It is a good idea to put in writing all relevant points, if relevant to your situation. *Date, sign, and copy* all documents you provide your lawyer for your safe-keeping and file organisation.

Also, get all of this in writing from your lawyer. Once you sign the costs agreement, you will be required to pay a retainer or deposit which goes into a special trust fund. Once invoices are sent to you and you approve them, money is withdrawn from this trust account by your lawyer to pay for legal services provided. And ensure you put this document and all documents in a file. Be sure to note their details in your Legal Services Log.

Cost agreements are vital to the effectiveness of your working relationship with your lawyer. They are an important instrument for preventing misunderstandings. Remember to ensure that regular updates are one of your requests documented in the agreement. The delivery of updates will ensure that you know that your matter is being attended to in a timely manner, that your lawyer is following your instructions, and both you and your lawyer are clear on the tasks that need to be done.

Summary of the contents of a Costs Agreement/Retainer

- the basis on which legal costs will be calculated
- the client's right to negotiate; receive a bill from the law practice; request an itemised account and be notified of any substantial change to any matter disclosed in the agreement
- an estimate of the total legal costs if practicable, or a range of estimates and an explanation of major variables that will affect the calculation of those costs
- details of intervals at which the client will be billed
- the rate of any interest, if any, that will be charged for overdue legal costs
- if a litigious matter, an estimate of the range of costs that may be recovered if the client is successful and the range of costs if the client is unsuccessful
- the client's right to progress reports including the progress of the matter and the costs incurred by the client to date
- details of the person whom the client may contact to discuss the legal costs; i.e. in the event of a dispute seeking a costs assessment and setting aside an agreement
- time limits to seek assessment.[89]

Be prepared to question your invoice

As you have just read, you, as a client, have the right, as all clients of lawyers do, to seek clarification of your invoice and the items listed as well as the time taken to complete tasks. You will recall that I reminded you earlier that creating a Legal Services Log was a great idea. This keeps you across all costs expenditure.

Consider asking your lawyer at the first appointment to attach to each invoice a copy of the applicable time-recording schedule for that invoice. Increasingly, law firms in some countries are providing clients with copies of their time-recording schedule and the invoice so that they can differentiate themselves from their competitors by demonstrating superior transparency. This innovation has a positive impact on client impressions and avoids client misunderstandings and reputational slights to the law firm involved. It is very important that you establish early in the process, if not almost immediately, what the process of dispute resolution will be. This question will alert the lawyer that you are aware that disputes may arise and you will be prepared to deal with them purposefully and assertively.

These days it is easy to be suspicious of over-billing given the negative perceptions of lawyer honesty. It may be that a simple mistake has occurred. Mistakes happen in every profession. It may well be a misunderstanding, but you won't know until you ask. And ask respectfully.

Accountability: Yours and your lawyer's

Being consumer aware means being alert to the many issues raised thus far in this book. Taking responsibility for your role as a client also involves a broad, if general, understanding of the legal profession. Let's take Australia and its legal profession as an example in point. Agencies have been established to regulate the legal profession and its professional practitioners. The professional conduct of lawyers is guided by the *Australian Solicitors Conduct Rules 2012*. The legal profession is underwritten by the legislation referred to as the *Legal Profession Act 2007* and is also guided by the body of the Law Council of Australia. The Legal Services Commission, which exists in most Australian states and territories, serves as the disciplinary and investigative regulatory body of the legal profession. You can refer to this body if you wish to make a complaint about over-billing or unethical conduct. All you need to do is refer to their website and contact them. Read information about lawyers and their role on your state's Law Society website. Regardless of the state/country you live in, your lawyer is accountable to the legal profession and oversight agencies such as those just mentioned.

Your lawyer has a duty to:

- act honestly and fairly in a client's best interests
- act with due skill and diligence, reasonable promptness and courtesy
- maintain a client's confidences
- avoid conflicts of interest
- communicate effectively and promptly with a client
- follow a client's lawful instructions.

In all states/countries like Australia, New Zealand, United Kingdom, Canada, and United States, you will be able to source an agency similar to the Legal Service Commission and a local Law Society. It is important for you, as a consumer, to know that agencies like these exist and that they play an important role in providing information and consumer protection. Taking your role as a client seriously means understanding this and having their contact details at hand. See the contact list for law societies at the end of this chapter.

Respect

Respect is a two-way street. Despite all of the scandal about predatory lawyers who act dishonestly, most lawyers are the opposite: caring, dedicated, knowledgeable and skilled practitioners of the law. Though your lawyer is professionally obliged to treat you with respect, your ethical obligations as a client require *you* to treat your lawyer with respect. This not only means providing information honestly, providing clear and timely instructions, and paying your bill on time, it means treating your lawyer as a professional who is experienced, skilled and qualified to help you. It means communicating clearly with them with substance and courtesy and not wasting their time. You will be a more effective client and a consumer-aware client if you make the effort to understand the role of your lawyer.

However, there is another side to this story.

Many of you might be surprised at the large number of clients who do the wrong thing by their lawyer. It is telling that companies have been established which are dedicated to collecting on bad debts for law firms because clients do not pay their bill. If you do not pay your bill your lawyer will simply cease working on your matter. If you have trouble paying your bill *be sure to communicate this to your lawyer.* Let them know your situation and together you can work out a way to meet your obligations. Teamwork can produce many a positive outcome. As this book has demonstrated, there are a number of valuable steps in saving money in your legal fee spending and crafting a highly workable relationship with your family lawyer.

Once you decide, act

Many a wise and ethical lawyer will tell you in no uncertain terms to act *promptly* should you start to lose faith in the lawyer you have retained. If an intractable issue arises for you in relation to your lawyer, take action. It is wise to advise your lawyer in writing that you are ending the arrangement with them. Consider the following example:

Dear ___

This email is to advise you that I am dissatisfied with your performance as my lawyer. I have repeatedly had to follow up on tasks that you had earlier indicated to me had been completed. I wish to make it clear that your failure to follow up on my instructions also amounts to failing to progress my matter.

I find this situation unacceptable. It is cause for me to retain another lawyer which I have now done. Her name is ______________. Since my invoices have all been paid I would appreciate you transferring my file to my new lawyer by immediate courier. Her address for delivery is ______________.

I look forward to hearing from my new lawyer that she has taken receipt of my file by the close of business today.

Yours faithfully

____

The moment when you decide that this lawyer is not right for you, *take the step of getting another lawyer.* Do not feel you are being held hostage by your lawyer (as many clients have told me that they have) since you have commenced working with them. Make sure you have paid all fees owed to your lawyer and request your lawyer to *immediately* have your file transferred to your *new* lawyer.

The task of finding a new lawyer will likely be daunting, but if you continue on an unsatisfactory path with a lawyer you no longer trust, then this can turn out to be *decidedly expensive and stressful for you and those around you,* especially if your lawyer delays progress or messes up your matter in some way. *Remember your purpose.* Be determined to progress your matter as soon as possible. This will take a lot of the stress away from your situation and will help save you money in the process.

It is important that you understand that, at first, your new lawyer will need to get up to speed and read your transferred file. This will likely cost you some money to do so, but it is *not* wasted money. Rather, it is an *investment* in progressing your matter. Find out how much it will cost you for your new lawyer to get up to speed, especially if you are further along in the process rather than at the beginning. Be sure to make clear to your new lawyer the reasons for sacking your previous lawyer so that your new lawyer is clear about your priorities. Some lawyers may agree to waive the fee for getting up to speed, so do ask about this possibility. If they agree to waive this fee, make sure that this waiver is included in your new cost agreement. That is to say, document and copy everything, including the reasons for your dissatisfaction with your previous family lawyer. The key is, of course, to act promptly on your decision to dispense with the lawyer you no longer trust.

Consider the following script for a favourable outcome:

> ***You:*** *Thank you for seeing me. I have done my research and understand you have a reputation for being very efficient in reaching settlement.*
>
> ***New Lawyer:*** *Thank you. That is good to hear. Smooth sailing to settlement*

is the best outcome for client and lawyer. I have received your file. I have also received your letter explaining why you have chosen new arrangements for your legal services. Thankfully you were not too far into your matter before you concluded your arrangement with your former lawyer. And it didn't take me long to review your file so let's forget about the fee for doing that, shall we?

You: *Thank you. I appreciate that.*

New Lawyer: *We need to focus on the outcomes you want and the best way to achieve them.*

Independent costs assessment

As well as retaining the services of a new lawyer, there are other measures you can take. If your dissatisfaction with your previous lawyer relates to costs and you think your lawyer overcharged you, you can apply for an independent costs assessment. You will be charged a fee for this and the services by the Assessor. First, however, inform your local Law Society.

Please note, though, given that time-based billing still seems to prevail in most law firms, the amount of time the lawyer has genuinely spent on completing a task for your matter is difficult to prove. Moreover, it is difficult to challenge the testing of the complaint given that the Independent Cost Assessor will be seeking to establish that the work completed was necessary and the time for which you were invoiced was reasonable. That is why, when you are looking for a lawyer to work with, you should *not* immediately choose the lawyer who charges the lowest hourly rate. It could end in disaster for you.

Conclusion

Making sure that you are across the consumer aspects of your legal services will go a long way to reducing your stress about legal fees. Moreover, your confidence in your ability to manage the situation effectively will likely improve as you navigate your separation. Bumps in the road? Address them and keep moving forward.

Law Societies

Australia, New Zealand, United Kingdom, Canada and America

Australia	
Law Society of the Australian Capital Territory	www.actlawsociety.asn.au
Queensland Law Society	www.qls.com.au
Law Institute of Victoria	www.liv.asn.au
Law Society of New South Wales	www.lawsociety.com.au
Law Society of South Australia	www.lawsocietysa.asn.au
Law Society of Tasmania	www.lst.org.au
Law Society of Western Australia	www.lawsocietywa.asn.au
Law Society of the Northern Territory	www.lawsocietynt.asn.au
New Zealand	
Law Society New Zealand	www.lawsociety.org.nz
United Kingdom	
Law Society of England and Wales	www.lawsociety.org.uk
Canada	
Federation of Law Societies	www.flsc.ca
United States	
American Law Society	americanlawsociety.com

SECTION 5
CHOOSING THE RIGHT FAMILY LAWYER FOR YOU

17

Choosing the right family lawyer for you

This book began by telling you that your choice of lawyer is crucial. Why? Because *the qualities of your family lawyer can make a favourable difference to your legal spend and outcomes.* The purpose of this chapter is to encourage you to consider the qualities of a family lawyer that *you* identify as important in getting you across the finishing line with resources for your future. But it's not all about your lawyer. It's about you too. Understanding that there is a working relationship between you and your lawyer is important. And it is one that you should closely monitor. Being a purposefully self-aware client is essential to the legal efficiency of your separation. Your understanding of the necessary aspects of your working relationship with your lawyer can save you money as well as separation delay.

This chapter offers you opportunities to understand:

- factors which influence your choice of lawyer
- that both lawyer and client have important roles to play
- qualities that can progress the efficient completion of your separation

What is your purpose?

Choosing the right family lawyer for you in such a confusing environment is challenging but consider my definition of 'a lawyer with whom you can work' as follows:

The best lawyer to work with is:

a lawyer whom you assess as a skilled, financially savvy, sound communicator who makes clear to you the complex concepts involved in your matter, who is empathic, who will not overcharge you, and who can help you achieve your goals in the least amount of time with the least amount of expense.

In sum, this client–lawyer working relationship is likely to be *ongoing*, so you need to be comfortable with them and confident in the lawyer's skill, efficiency, and honesty.

So, how do you find the right lawyer for you? Do you do what many clients do, and conduct an internet search for 'family lawyers' in your area? Check the relevant state's Law Society directory of family lawyers? Do you accept the recommendation of a friend? Do you take the advice of a doctor, crisis service worker, or financial advisor or accountant you have worked with? All of these methods are feasible, but any of them can land you in difficulty if the lawyer you have chosen is *not* right for you. Before you choose your method of finding a family lawyer it is a good idea to make a list of goals for your process. After that, consider the best legal option for concluding your relationship.

By this stage, you will have read about the core legal options for your process. You may have already decided the option you prefer, given your separation circumstances and the personalities involved. Which option are you leaning towards?

How you want to proceed will influence your choice of family lawyer. For instance, if you want to conduct your settlement using the collaborative law process, the lawyer you will need to choose should be trained in collaborative law and be a very skilled negotiator. Or if you prefer lawyer-assisted negotiation, they will need to have a high rate of efficient settlement.

Experience and accreditation

When choosing a family lawyer, many clients tend to view public recognition of professional skill as a predictor of a positive outcome in their settlement. Many people feel reassured by a high level of specialist skills and long years of experience. Many of you will be prepared to pay more for a lawyer who has advanced skill levels which are recognised by their professional body, such as your state's Law Society or Bar Association. For instance, in Australia, a family lawyer with recognised advanced skill levels is referred to as an Accredited Family Law Specialist. To be clear about what this advanced level of skill and experience entails, it is worth looking briefly at this issue.

In Australia, for example, an Accredited Family Law Specialist must have worked in family law for a minimum of five years to be eligible to sit for a rigorous exam to demonstrate advanced family law skill. They are then required to maintain their high standard through annual professional development.

Similar advanced measures are recognised in the United Kingdom, Canada, New Zealand and the United States. The Law Society website of the state/country in which you reside will have a list of Accredited Family Law Specialists or their equivalents. Even so, retaining an Accredited Family Law Specialist will not guarantee that your lawyer is the right lawyer for *you*.

Nevertheless, regardless of how much knowledge you have at this stage of your separation process, it is very likely that you will have in your mind expectations about your lawyer. It is to these expectations we now turn.

You and your preferences

There will be other qualities you may prefer your family lawyer to possess. What are your expectations of your lawyer's professional and interpersonal traits? What expectations do you have of the outcomes to be achieved by your lawyer? Expectations and your own failure to manage them can lead to misunderstandings, further expense and heightened stress (for both you and your lawyer), all of which will interfere with the clarity of your decision-making. Good decision-making = saving money.

Which of the following are your preferred qualities of the family lawyer you seek? Ask yourself some tough questions and respond honestly. This 'audit' process helps you stay on track in thinking purposefully about choosing the right lawyer for you.

Tick whichever requirements listed below apply to you. Do you want your lawyer to:

- ☐ be able to clearly explain complicated issues so that you can understand them?
- ☐ be aggressive towards the other party and get you the results you want no matter what?
- ☐ be up for a fight, none of this cooperative business; no 'softly, softly' rubbish?
- ☐ be financially astute?
- ☐ be resourceful and think about clever strategy to get you the best settlement?
- ☐ understand that they provide a service where you bark and they bite?
- ☐ be someone who protects your interests and encourages you to stand your ground?
- ☐ be totally results-focused rather than time-based in their billing?
- ☐ be totally transparent about costs, including informing you of payment schedules and manner of payment?
- ☐ follow your instructions whether they are lawful or not?
- ☐ listen to you moan and groan for most of the appointment?
- ☐ provide an easy-to-understand costs agreement or contract for services?
- ☐ be able to explain your options for managing your separation in a way that you can understand?

- ☐ point out the expenses, benefits and weaknesses of options available to you?
- ☐ advise you of the short and long-term cost of your actions?
- ☐ be alert to misleading or false information provided by the other party, especially financial information?
- ☐ not be unnecessarily adversarial, but reasonable and proportionate?
- ☐ appreciate that you want to finalise your property settlement and parenting arrangements effectively but also efficiently. That it is imperative that matters be resolved as quickly as possible?
- ☐ keep you updated as progress happens?
- ☐ inform you of any changes which may impact on your costs?
- ☐ be available and responsive to your enquiries in a timely manner?

Now, pause for a moment and reflect. Did any of these requirements resonate with you? Which ones? *Why* are they important to you? Are there qualities that are not included in the list? Which ones? Why are these other qualities important to you?

It is worth making some notes about this 'self-audit' while reflecting on your responses. Consider using this exercise to clarify your thinking about the kind of lawyer you wish to retain, as well as the type of working relationship you develop together.

Insight: LGBTIQ+ clients and culturally competent lawyers

Key to understanding that many factors may impact on relationship collapse is recognising that relationships come in all shapes and sizes, all backgrounds, and have dynamics which may be distinct to them. In view of society's general lack of understanding of the lived experiences of people who identify as

LGBTIQ+, I have chosen to use this book to also foster the understanding of issues relevant to a section of the population deemed a 'minority'. If you identify as LGBTIQ+, these factors may reflect your experience and/or your confusion. Most especially, these factors should be understood by your family lawyer. Such knowledge and understanding can prevent problems, delay, and can enhance the quality of the client-lawyer teamwork.

The purpose of this insight is to draw out some of the issues that are likely to be unique to same-sex and gender diverse clients when dealing with your lawyer. While some lawyers themselves identify as LGBTIQ+, many do not. Furthermore, bigotry is alive and well in the legal profession, as it is in any other profession. And there are lawyers who are hostile to individuals who do not live the heterosexually structured lives that they themselves do. It is important to name the beliefs held by some service providers so that you, as a family law client, can be alert to signs that the lawyer you have chosen may not possess the understanding and empathy to provide the experience you need.

Behaviours of service providers who do not understand LGBTIQ+ issues include but are not limited to:

- knowing and unknowing discrimination against clients from same sex and gender diverse backgrounds
- an assumption that intimate partner violence is just like that of heterosexual relationships
- an assumption that intimate partner violence is mutual in LGBTIQ+ relationships
- lack of awareness and sensitivity to strategies used by abusers
- that LGBTIQ+ experience discrimination, or fear of discrimination, particularly from police and the criminal justice system – the legal system in general which includes family law
- an assumption that in lesbian relationships women are not capable of exerting physical power over women

- assumptions that gay men are not 'masculine' and are therefore not capable of exerting physical power over their partner.[90]

Let's get a clear idea of the behaviours identified by researchers that can occur in same-sex and gender diverse separations. I should point out that researchers have found that many of the abusive behaviours that occur in heterosexual relationships, typically perpetrated by men against women, can be found in relationships between same-sex and gender-diverse relationships.

However, there are behaviours that are unique to intimate partner violence in same-sex and gender diverse relationships. Social exclusion is often part of the lived experience of people in same-sex and gender diverse relationships. Behaviours identified by researchers that are unique to abusive LGBTIQ+ partners that your lawyer should be aware of, and accommodate in their strategic management of your matter, include some of the following:

- abusive partners may use phobia or heterosexism to exercise power and control over their partner, e.g. 'outing' or threats to 'out' their partner's sexuality or HIV status
- perpetrators may use their partner's sexuality or identity as a form of control by limiting their access to friends and social networks, or by threatening to tell their partner's employer, parent, children, landlord or friends
- coercive control of partners through actions or threats which may result in the loss of children, employment, relationship or housing
- abusive partners can suggest to the other partner that they will not be believed if they lodge complaints with police or health services and that they will be discriminated against
- generally, the fear of isolation and homophobia within the broader community can contribute to victims staying with abusive partners
- confusion by victims, especially lesbian women, regarding intimate

partner violence since it is typically understood as perpetrated by men against women

- some lesbian abusers of their partners will present as victims to shelters and support groups to continue the abuse against their partner by chasing and stalking them in these spaces or by making it impossible for their partner to seek support from these services
- confusion by gay men regarding the power relations of intimate partner violence, especially when it involves rape.[91]

There may be times when you cannot access a lawyer who is appropriately skilled and informed about the lived experiences and relationships of same-sex and gender diverse people. So, what do you do? How do you handle this situation? How do you prepare? What do you say to a lawyer who appears to have little idea about important factors of same-sex or sexually diverse relationships and their breakups? Here's the thing. You have choices. Options are open to you if you have difficulty in accessing a culturally competent lawyer to assist you with your separation.

- Ask around about lawyers who have a positive reputation for knowledge and understanding of issues which are unique to same-sex and gender-diverse relationships or who, themselves, openly identify as LGBTIQ+ and welcome LGBTIQ+ clients.
- Like many people who are not included in mainstream service design, you can accept the burden of educating your lawyer in your first consultation. While you will likely be stressed and juggling several issues in your head, you will have the life experience to know whether this lawyer is right for you. Do they seem genuine? Their questions about your relationship and its collapse will give you a clue.
- You are not compelled to see your lawyer face-to-face. You can access a culturally competent lawyer online via Skype, Zoom, FaceTime, telephone, or by using other conferencing technologies. If it is difficult transport-wise, parenting-wise, financially, disability-wise, or employment-wise and your preferred lawyer practises anywhere

in the same state in which you live, you can still retain their services. Technology can be your ally.

You are not alone. You have options. Explore them.

Conclusion

Misunderstandings between clients and lawyers can often result from a clash between your expectations of your lawyer, expectations regarding the outcomes of your first consultation, expectations of what you can achieve, and the discomfort of not having total control over your legal process. Being a self-aware client will help prevent expensive misunderstandings. Let's now turn to the issue of how to communicate clearly with your lawyer.

18

Communicating effectively with your lawyer

Communication lies at the heart of most things in life. How *well* you communicate can make a big difference to the amount of money you spend on legal fees. It is essential that you think carefully about how you communicate with your lawyer and how you want your lawyer to communicate with you. Earlier, I mentioned that this dynamic means that you need to appreciate that the arrangement between service provider and client is *teamwork*. This will help you make the job of your lawyer easier which, in the long run, will mean you pay less in legal fees. And *you* have a responsibility to understand this. The purpose of this chapter is to canvas key factors which can help you craft a productive working relationship with your lawyer. Reflecting on your first consultation with your lawyer will help make you sharp.

This chapter offers you opportunities to understand:

- that communication efficiency between you and your lawyer will save you money and time
- the value of the chronological briefing of your lawyer
- the purpose of your first consultation with your family lawyer
- key issues to address in your first consultation
- how to assess if the lawyer with whom you have your first consultation is 'right' for you

Your first consultation

Your discussions with your lawyer will almost always be in their office unless by remote technology such as zoom, facetime, skype, etc. It will be structured by the to-and-fro of questions and answers. Be sure to remember that your first consultation with a family lawyer does *not* oblige you to continue the relationship. You have no obligations to satisfy until you have signed the Costs Agreement/Retainer. Ultimately, the purpose of your first consultation with a family lawyer is information gathering, gaining initial advice, and assessing the lawyer. Note also that even if you decide to work with the first family lawyer you consult and realise soon after that it was *not* a good idea, all you need to do is ensure that your payment of your account is current and notify the lawyer that you wish to exit the relationship. This issue was discussed earlier in chapter sixteen.

Your family lawyer is there to provide you with services so that you can finalise the end of your relationship, reach a fair settlement and, if minor aged children are involved, formalise parenting arrangements. To do this, your lawyer needs information about you. This information was discussed in chapter two (your Ex, the breakdown in the relationship, children, contributions, assets and liabilities). Your lawyer will provide you with advice in response to the information you provide, and any questions you have.

In turn, you need to inform your lawyer of your priorities and how you want your lawyer to handle matters. You do not need to provide instructions at your first appointment. You may prefer to digest the advice given. It is imperative that your lawyer understands what you want to achieve and how. For your lawyer to be able to do this, you need to be clear about what you want.

Communicate clearly

A good family lawyer will be skilled at making people feel relaxed and help their client articulate their concerns. In reality, both parties have a responsibility to communicate clearly to the other. Here's what you can do to get your message across.

Thinking about *how* you can present your thoughts during your appointment with your lawyer is an important task in your preparation for the legal process, and for the process of working with your lawyer efficiently.

Ensure that you present your information to your lawyer chronologically. Try setting out a chronological timeline with dates and key details. Provide your lawyer with a copy. Place a copy of this timeline in your filing system. Also consider your verbal presentation. For instance, many people speak rapidly and present their thoughts out of order and even forget to address key issues. How can you expect your lawyer to quickly decipher the relevant information upon which to base their advice to you? As part of your preparation, why not rehearse with a friend? Practise what you want to say to your lawyer, speaking at at a measured pace and breathing evenly while doing so. Other questions might occur to you during your rehearsing which you can add to your list of issues you want to raise.

Your lawyer will also have questions for you. Consider your responses to the following questions: Why did your relationship end? What were the issues of conflict between you and your Ex prior to your relationship end? What is the level of conflict now? Who are the key parties?

If you are not sure whom the lawyer might consider to be a key party, provide a comprehensive list of people and their contact details. These parties will typically include you, your Ex, your parents, the parents of your Ex, siblings of either you or your Ex (if they are involved in contact with your children), the parents of your children's friends, their school teachers/sports coach, or childcare centre director, your children's doctor, and your neighbours.

It will help if you write your responses down to read and re-read what you have written. Have the courage to be honest with yourself. Let's say your lawyer asks you why your relationship ended. While you may know and have spent time thinking about the reasons, do not feel pressured to tell your lawyer straightaway. Do not feel pressured to provide intimate details if you are not comfortable doing so at your first appointment. But at some stage you will need to fully inform your lawyer. They need that information to do their job effectively.

Provide clear instructions to your lawyer

Having established that clearly instructing your lawyer is important, let's unpack the issuing of instructions. 'Instructions' is a legal term which refers to the directions you provide your lawyer about the services you want delivered. Here are five suggestions you might like to consider when preparing yourself to instruct your lawyer.

1. Try to instruct your lawyer only after you have done your best to make sure they are the right lawyer for you; that you have a sense that your lawyer genuinely appreciates the approach you want to take and understands your priorities; that you are clear about the limits of what your lawyer can achieve for you, and that all of your doubts and questions have been addressed; and that you feel comfortable and in control of your case.
2. Instruct your lawyer *in person* if at all possible. Some clients find providing instructions via telephone uncertain. You can use Skype, FaceTime, Zoom, or whatever conferencing technology is available to you if you cannot see your lawyer in person. This will be important for people who are housebound, have a particular disability, and those who reside in a rural or remote location. And let's not forget that Covid-19 is now endemic and future pandemics are anticipated. Put everything in writing and copy it.
3. If it is appropriate to your situation and you are afraid that your stress will prevent you from absorbing the advice your lawyer gives you, bring a family member or friend along. Ensure, however, that they do not interfere in any way in the content of your instructions to your lawyer. They may think they are acting in your best interests, but remember, this is *your* case.
4. Make sure that you have provided your instructions clearly. Read them from your notes, if you wish. It is very important that you check with your lawyer that they understand your instructions. Ask your lawyer to provide you with feedback regarding the consequences of your instructions so there are no nasty or unexpected outcomes that

you have not foreseen. Throughout the process, it is a good idea to revisit your instructions and continually clarify with your lawyer any issue which may confuse you.

5. If there appears to be a limit to what your lawyer can achieve for you, make sure that you find out why. Always try to understand what is going on so there are no misunderstandings. Misunderstandings, if not resolved as soon as possible, cost money.

Once you retain your lawyer, you are entitled to what is known as 'lawyer–client confidentiality'. *Everything* you say to your lawyer is confidential, so do not beat about the bush or spend time masking your own indiscretions, poor conduct, or trying to cover your embarrassment at having to discuss such intimate issues with a stranger. Be honest. The reality is that lawyers have heard it all before. No matter how embarrassed you may be, do not stray from telling your lawyer the truth. Do *not* mislead them.

Lawyers must comply with relevant statutory obligations and the rules of the legal profession. These rules include not misleading the Court, or your former partner's lawyer, and not acting unlawfully. So, as tempting as it might be to retaliate, especially when your Ex behaves badly, be sure to never expect your lawyer to deceive 'the other side' because there is no 'other side'.

It is all too easy to get sidetracked during your appointment with your lawyer. It helps to steadfastly remain focused on getting answers to your questions (which you have on paper in front of you) and listen to the advice your lawyer is providing. Apart from brief social courtesy, get to the point and deal with the task at hand. Your lawyer is not your friend with whom you chat about your social life. Nor is your lawyer your therapist, on whom you unload your emotional angst or vent about your former partner. Departing from the business at hand will cost you money, and over time it will cost you *lots of money*. Staying on point will help you avoid unnecessary expense.

Assess your lawyer

If you wish to purposefully assess whether the family lawyer you choose to consult for your first appointment is right for you, then you would be wise to ask them several questions. And please note that there are many fine family lawyers across many states/countries who agree on the wisdom of the following suggestions.

Settlement success rate

If you are seeking to reach a settlement with your former partner as soon as possible and as inexpensively as possible, then consider asking the lawyer what their 'settlement success rate' is, in particular:

- How has the lawyer performed?
- What percentage of this lawyer's clients has the lawyer assisted in reaching an early settlement?
- What was the typical timeframe?
- What has their success rate been in high conflict settlements?

Approach to family law

You should ask the lawyer about their approach to family law and whether they have a preferred approach. You will be familiar with the options from earlier chapters. Moreover, ensure that you follow up by asking your lawyer what the respective costs and benefits of their preferred approach are and whether their preference is related to the strengths they identify as having as a lawyer. As blunt as this may sound, your settlement process requires some fortitude on your part.

After informing the lawyer of your own situation, ask the lawyer how they think it best to address your matter; whether they have a recommended plan in mind; whether they have a timeframe in which to achieve the goals you have outlined; and whether or not your lawyer thinks that your goals are achievable in a reasonably short timeframe, provided the other party is cooperative (remembering, of course, that it only takes *one* party to obstruct and delay).

Who does your work?

If you are concerned that the lawyer may be very busy and likely to delegate your matter to a junior staff member, then be sure to ask them whether or not they do. If this issue is important to you, make it very clear that you do not want this to happen. Your dollars are precious to your future financial security and you simply must spend them wisely. Moreover, if you are paying fees for work done by junior staff, you should expect to be invoiced for work conducted at junior staff rates.

Consider the following script:

> ***You:*** *I am sure you will understand that I have no wish to spend more money than I need to on this matter.*
>
> ***Lawyer:*** *Of course.*
>
> ***You:*** *It is important to me that I understand everything about the costs for services. Will you be working on my case or will there be others? I want to avoid being in a situation where I am paying everyone the same rate I am paying you. I don't believe that's fair. I'd like my invoices from you to be itemised and clearly indicate who has worked on which task. That way there will be no misunderstandings.*
>
> ***Lawyer:*** *I understand what you are saying, ____. I will do my level best to make sure that that happens. If you have questions about any invoices just ask.*
>
> ***You:*** *I'd like an explanation as soon as possible and I don't want to be paying for the time spent receiving an answer.*
>
> ***Lawyer:*** *I hear you.*
>
> ***You:*** *Thank you.*

To some of you this script might seem overly assertive. It is not. It is clear communication to your lawyer regarding billing expectations. It also puts your lawyer on notice that you expect efficiency and transparency, and a determination to get your separation finalised without fuss from the lawyer who is representing you.

Beware of the six-minute unit

The time you spend with your lawyer, whether in person, on the telephone, reading emails, returning messages or whatever, costs money. As mentioned earlier in this book, time-based billing has become increasingly controversial and has led to many a complaint with regulatory agencies which oversee lawyer conduct. Thankfully, innovations in the legal services market which promote transparency in client billing are becoming a welcome feature.

Beware of this time-based billing if you are seeking to be careful with your legal fee spending. In some states/countries many lawyers still charge by six-minute units—a tenth of an hour. Even when a task might take them two minutes, you will likely be billed for the six-minute unit. This practice is referred to as 'rounding up'. To point out the obvious, these units add up. Think about this for a moment. When you telephone your lawyer for a brief question or email them, this could cost you AU$40 to AU$70 or more, depending on the hourly rate your lawyer charges. These 'brief' tasks can very quickly add up. If your separation takes several months or a couple of years to finalise (despite the best intentions of the Court), and if you do not communicate with your lawyer with this time-billing in mind, including 'brief' contacts, then you could easily be looking at many thousands of dollars! This is money you can avoid spending. This is money best reserved for funding your future choices in life.

Keep your lawyer informed

Ensure that your lawyer has *current* information. Shape your role as a client to make your lawyer's job as easy as possible. If your circumstances change, for example if you move house, change your telephone number, and so on, be sure to let your lawyer know. This change in circumstances may be likely since family law matters can take several months to be finalised. If your lawyer has to research your new whereabouts or take time in finding out where to contact you, this will cost you money. It will also delay completion of your legal process. You will need to stay in contact with your lawyer to monitor progress.

You will likely have taken your documents file to your first appointment with your lawyer. If your lawyer requires further information from you or more documents, ensure that you provide your lawyer the information required as soon as possible. You can help yourself and your lawyer by asking at your first consultation for a list of any other information needed and *deadlines* which apply so you can schedule your tasks if need be. Be sure to meet deadlines set. If your matter involves Court hearings, then ensure that your diary includes your schedule of Court hearings. Be early and *never, ever be late.* Court-based activity is very expensive and if your lawyer is required to seek a continuance because you have not arrived on time, then your legal costs will balloon. If documents are needed urgently or have a filing deadline, then get them to your lawyer at your earliest opportunity.

Reflect: how does your lawyer behave?

Reflect on your first consultation. After your first consultation with your lawyer, you will be well positioned to assess whether your lawyer is the right lawyer for *you*. With the previous chapters in mind, you will be now aware of your expectations of your lawyer, you will have reflected on whether your expectations are reasonable, and you will know that there is a professional standard of conduct lawyers must meet in their consultations with clients. After your first consultation with your family lawyer, why not spend some time reflecting on their *demonstrated behaviour* during the consultation? This will assist you in making a choice of lawyer you can be satisfied with.

Why not ask yourself the following questions? Indicate your response to the questions you find relevant to your circumstances.

Assess your Lawyer

Question	Yes/No
Do they listen to you?	
Are they responsive to your questions?	
Are they clearly adversarial and warrior battle-seeking?	
Is this your case or theirs?	
Do they understand diversity?	
Do they exhibit homophobia or other biases?	
Do they clearly explain complex concepts so that you can understand what is going on and what may happen?	
Do they clearly explain the process and your options, so that you can understand and take an active and leading role in your process?	
Do they welcome questions from you?	
Do they cut you off and prevent you from finishing what you wanted to say (because they 'have seen this situation before')?	
Are they empathetic or autocratic or dictatorial or dismissive in their manner towards you?	
Are they upfront about their costs?	
How do they seem to express their negotiation skills?	
Do they treat you with respect or are they condescending?	
Does their language suggest an approach to family law that is contrary to what they have told you?	
Do they appear overly busy and likely to delegate matters to a junior member of staff?	

Conclusion

Put your issues on the table so you are both working from the same page. Communicate clearly. Communicate with purpose. You may discover that your comfort with your lawyer grows as your lawyer demonstrates their knowledge, skill and willingness to listen to you during your consultation. Or you may discover qualities during your first consultation that are red flags and require action. It is worth going through this reflection exercise since it can help you save money on your legal spending.

Whatever you do, move forward.

19

What are *your* qualities as a client?

This chapter focuses on how your communication style, your personality and your expectations of your lawyer impact *your* ability to work efficiently with your lawyer and save money on legal fees. The exercise of reflecting on *your own behaviour* in a context in which family lawyers are often vilified may seem novel to you. This exercise, however, is worth completing. It will help steer your communication in the right direction with insight from within the legal profession. Such self-awareness will fuel sound behaviour.

This chapter offers you opportunities to understand:

- the impact of poor client behaviour on the working relationship between you and your lawyer
- client behaviours considered 'difficult' by many lawyers

Self-audit

It may be that the preferred qualities you seek in your family lawyer are linked to one or more of the qualities *you* yourself have. Thus, engaging in self-reflection would likely be helpful when approaching the task of choosing a family lawyer. What are your personality traits? Why not reflect on your emotional resilience? Where are your strengths? Where are your vulnerabilities? Self-awareness boosts the effectiveness of decision-making.

Now think about *your own* qualities and their potential consequences.

What Type of Client Will You Be?

Questions	Yes/No
Are you impatient?	
Are you overly compliant?	
Do you have any fears? If so, name them.	
Are you overwhelmed by stress?	
Are you prone to anger?	
Have you lost all trust in the sincerity of your Ex's communication and negotiation attempts?	
Are you despairing of your Ex's refusal to cooperate and simply want to give them want they want just to get rid of them?	
Do you suffer from anxiety and/or depression?	
Are you vulnerable to quick compromises in order to end the stress and have the whole mess done and dusted?	
Do you suffer from alcohol and/or other drug addiction?	
Are other factors clouding your judgement?	
Are you fearful of your sexuality being outed?	
Are you overwhelmed by your lack of financial literacy?	
Are you in need of psychological counselling to cope with the process of legal formalities of concluding your relationship?	
Are you honest with yourself about the reasons your relationship with your Ex broke down?	
Will you educate yourself about the issues involved?	
Are you easily intimidated?	
Are you vulnerable to letting your lawyer run the show?	
Do you take responsibility for your own actions and decisions?	
Are you expecting or aware of leverage being used against you?	

Questions	Yes/No
Are you exposed to emotional bullying or blackmail by your older children?	
Are you afraid of your Ex, and does that fear impact your expectations of your lawyer?	

Reflect on your responses. Think about how these qualities may impact those around you. Think especially about how the qualities you have identified above can affect your interaction with your lawyer.

Make sure you are not a 'difficult' client

Think also about whether or not your expectations of your lawyer are *reasonable*. The legal profession is generally a very stressful one. Alcohol and other drug abuse, depression and suicide amongst lawyers are recognised problems due to work stress. While there are many factors which contribute to undermining lawyers' wellbeing, the one I wish to raise in this context is high conflict clients. Most clients are positive and exemplary clients who do their best to work with their lawyer to resolve their matter. 'Difficult' clients are perceived by lawyers to demonstrate one, some, or many of the following behaviours (this list is not exhaustive, but you may consider circling the ones that resonate with you).

Behaviours of a difficult client

- refusing to consider carefully the lawyer's advice
- being emphatically unrealistic in your expectations
- being inflexible
- contacting your lawyer about irrelevant matters
- repeatedly insisting on giving your lawyer unnecessary information
- refusing to take responsibility for your matter and blaming others

- being vengeful in your instructions
- continually obsessing about the other party's responsibility for the relationship breakup
- being emotionally erratic
- continually expressing doubt about your lawyer's reasonable advice
- complaining about the work conducted by your lawyer when it has been clearly satisfactory
- behaving as if you know more about the law than the lawyer when you clearly do not
- demanding that the lawyer behave unlawfully.

In sum, a high conflict, difficult client is one who is demanding, unrealistic, erratic, controlling and impossible to please. Such a high conflict client refuses to take responsibility for their behaviour, and demonstrates manipulative, vengeful and adversarial conduct.

When a lawyer has a high conflict client, the environment can rapidly become unproductive for both client and lawyer. Misunderstandings can easily arise. Communication suffers because the lawyer has the added burden of communicating in a manner designed to manage your high conflict demeanour, rather than progressing your matter efficiently.

In short, a high conflict client can easily incur greater legal expense and thus make the separation process more expensive. *Difficult clients tend to sabotage their own case.* Make sure that this is not you. It is a reality that when you are under significant stress, you are vulnerable to behaving badly. Adverse situations do tend to bring out the worst in most people. With this in mind, try to remember to be kind to yourself *and* to your lawyer.

Be aware, however, that your lawyer has every right to 'sack' you as a client. They can refuse your retainer because of your unreasonable behaviour. If this does occur, then you will need to go back to the drawing board and spend more time, more money and endure greater stress seeking new counsel because your case has not been resolved and will now take longer. You have, as they say, 'shot yourself in the foot'. And no-one wants to be in this position, least of all you.

Conclusion

The issues raised in this chapter may well have been confronting for you. However, I believe that being self-aware and conducting 'self-audits' will help you be a more confident, effective client who deals with their lawyer in a focused and clear manner. This will very likely help you save on your legal spend and complete the legal aspects of your separation sooner rather than later.

SECTION 6
HELP

20
Where to find help

Seek help when you need it. When you do this you come closer to finalising your separation. This chapter introduces you to the professionals who work in the area of family law, relationship separation, and divorce. There are, of course, many other professionals who specialise in resolving the particular issues which emerge in your separation situation. I have identified the main types of professionals upon whom you can draw.

This chapter offers you opportunities to understand:

- the notion of help-seeking
- differences in help-seeking by different groups of people
- the array of professionals who can help you during your separation
- the work that these professionals do and how to use their services

Seeking help

You might be surprised at how many people are wary about asking for help. I used to be one of them. What is the worst that can happen if you ask someone for help? They can say 'no'. You might be offended, but at least you asked. But there is more to the story of help-seeking.

What is help-seeking? To ensure that we are on the same page, let's be clear about what help-seeking actually is. Researchers agree that help-seeking is the action of searching for resources outside of ourselves to achieve a task or solve a problem. One of Australia's most essential helping organisations, Lifeline, puts it simply as: 'the process of finding and receiving help from others'.[92] Lifeline tells people that help is easier to find than people might think. It combats beliefs that inhibit people from seeking help, such as:

- thinking a problem will go away on its own
- feeling afraid or embarrassed to ask for help
- thinking that no one will want to help
- thinking that no one understands
- not knowing where to go to find help
- a lack of support services in your area
- thinking that professionals will judge you
- thinking that getting help will be expensive or time-consuming.[93]

The fear of appearing stupid, and the fear of being seen as weak, sit high on the list of reasons why people find it difficult to ask others for help. So, too, does the fear of appearing to be out of control of your life, being a burden to someone, and owing them a favour. Psychologists agree these factors play a strong role in undermining help-seeking behaviour.

Effective help-seeking is when a person knows *when* they need help, the *kind* of help they need, *whom* to ask for help, and *how* to ask for the help that is needed.

Women are more willing than men to seek help. While men may be reluctant to ask for help so too are marginalised groups within society – which include women and men for different reasons than cited earlier. Asking for help maintains engagement, fosters independence and adjustment, helps avoid failure, and fosters self-regulation.

On the ground

The raw time of relationship separation is tough enough without you being afraid to ask for help. Let's have a look at some practical ways you can do this.

Sincerity and respect are important. If someone you ask for help in a respectful manner does not respond kindly, they are simply the wrong person. It is not about you. It is about them. Maybe they are having a bad day. Maybe they are not actually a helpful person. However, try to remember that most people will generally want to help you if they can. Mostly, it will be because it makes them feel better about themselves. And besides, the inner glow of kindness is inside most of us. And what's more, the person you have approached will very likely feel respected and trusted. That, in itself, is a positive experience for them.

The timing of your request for help is another factor to think about. Perhaps the people you need help from are only available on the weekends. Why not consider including the issue of time in your request? When you ask someone for help, give them a timeframe and be specific about when would be best. This improves your odds of getting the help you need.

Letting the other person know that you have already tried to fix the issue that you need help with before you ask them for their advice helps establish the groundwork for stronger social ties and goodwill. There is no need to go into great detail about your attempts. Get straight to the point.

When someone gives you the help you need and things work out well for you, be sure to give positive feedback to the person who has helped you. And even if the result you seek does not eventuate, the two words 'thank you' are the most powerful words to say in any case.

People are not mind-readers, so when you ask for help, be brief, straight to the point, and state clearly what it is you need help with and when and where. Turning your request for help into an irritatingly lengthy story will quickly push many people into compassion fatigue and they will likely apologise and declare that they are simply too busy to help.

Whether or not your request results in help, be gracious. Asking for help is an opportunity to improve your life. At the end of the day, remember that asking for help will likely result in feeling good and not disaster. What's more, by continually offering to help others and helping them with *their* problems, you will find it easier to ask for help with *yours*.

If you are someone who identifies as LGBTIQ+, you will likely know that other factors can make it difficult to seek help. Here, I want to add to the understanding of issues specific to same-sex and gender diverse relationship separation issues because they are so poorly understood.

Insight: LGBTIQ+ clients and barriers to help-seeking

One such factor is stigma. Stigma plays a powerful role in inhibiting the willingness of people who identify as LGBTIQ+ from seeking help.[94] The term, 'stigma' refers to the 'disapproval of, or discrimination against, a person based on perceived social characteristics that serve to distinguish them from other members of a society'.[95] It diminishes the wellbeing of people who live lives which differ from 'normalised' (heterosexual) behaviour. The impacts of stigma do serious psychological damage and undermine the success of relationships themselves. Research has found that few practitioners and help service providers are across relevant LGBTIQ+ issues, especially in rural/regional areas.[96] It is essential that your family lawyer be familiar with the impacts of stigma.

Some of the barriers to help seeking are listed below.[97]

Factors which contribute to LGBTIQ+ avoidance of help-seeking:

- the desire not to draw negative attention to LGBTIQ+ communities
- the risk of survivors being alienated within LGBTIQ+ communities
- the belief that their experience will not be taken seriously by police and police discrimination against them
- because they are not open with their sexual orientation or gender identity, especially if their family is unaware about their LGBTIQ+ status

- trans people might fear being 'outed' before they are ready to disclose their identity, and/or before they have made associated changes such as using preferred pronouns, a preferred name, changing physical appearance or undergoing any surgical procedures or hormonal therapies
- conversely, trans people who have been 'passing' as a particular gender may fear seeking help because this would expose their trans history
- an inability by support services/practitioners to view intimate partner violence outside of a heterosexual framework in which intimate partner violence is perpetrated by men against women — that intimate partner violence is just like that of heterosexual relationships
- a failure to recognise intimate partner violence because it does not resemble that in heterosexual relationships — an assumption that in lesbian relationships women are not capable of exerting physical power over women
- assumptions that gay men are not 'masculine' and are therefore not capable of exerting physical power over their partner
- an assumption that intimate partner violence is mutual in LGBTIQ+ relationships
- insensitivity to and/or lack of awareness of the specific needs/issues of relationships conducted by same-sex and gender diverse individuals
- lack of awareness and sensitivity to strategies used by abusers.

Sources of help

Who can help you when you separate? What sources of support are out there? In all the confusion of your separation, many of you do not know where to go, let alone what to do. If this sounds like you, then happy news. This section is dedicated to giving you this information. You are not alone in going through your separation. At the end of this chapter, you will find a list of some sources of help. Please draw on their expertise if you need to and are in a position to do so.

Family Lawyer

Throughout this book you will have learned much about family lawyers, their duties and obligations, and the ways to achieve the most value from their services. They are the key professionals to facilitate the outcome of your legal process. The difficulty in accessing legal aid is well known and governments in western legal systems receive constant advocacy for more resources for people who cannot afford legal services. Below you will find a list of contact details of legal aid services in Australia. Other countries such as New Zealand, United Kingdom, Canada and the United States will have similar agencies.

Legal Aid Offices in Australia

Legal Aid (national)		nla.aust.net.au
Australian Capital territory	1300 654314	legalaidact.org.au
New South Wales	1300 888529	legalaid.nsw.gov.au
Northern Territory	1800 019 343	ntlac.nt.gov.au
Queensland	1300 651 188	legalaid.qld.gov.au
South Australia	1300 366 424	lsc.sa.gov.au
Tasmania	1300 366 611	legalaid.tas.gov.au
Victoria	1300 792 387	legalaid.vic.gov.au
Western Australia	1300 650 579	legalaid.wa.gov.au

Family doctor/family physician/general practitioner (GP)

If you have a good doctor who takes an active approach to your primary care, then you already have one of the most important resources you will need throughout the completion of your separation. Doctors are a practical source of help with their own medical expertise, to dispense scripts for medication that some of you may need for your stress-related illness, and to provide referrals to medical specialists.

Also, some doctors are specially trained in stress management and therapeutic counselling. They can also put you in touch with effective clinical psychologists. I take my hat off to conscientious doctors. Doctors can be a crucial source of help in separation situations. People tend to find good doctors through personal recommendation and location directories. Be sure to have a list of contact details of your doctor handy. Consider including the contact details of a back-up doctor for when your own doctor is away.

If your separation is causing you to feel highly stressed, unable to make decisions or relate to others, has arrested your ability to cope at work or studies, or if you feel overwhelmed, your doctor can help you further by working with you to create a Mental Health Care Plan, should you reside in Australia.

What is a Mental Health Care Plan? It is a plan created by you with your doctor and it is one you need to steer, just like you steer your interaction with your lawyer. Working on a plan with your doctor takes longer than a normal appointment so be sure to book a long appointment with the receptionist. During your appointment with your doctor discuss your concerns honestly. If you have trouble giving names to feelings or experiences, try describing them in the most basic terms. Your doctor will have encountered patients with this challenge before. It is really important to be honest about what is going on for you. Forget being embarrassed. Doctors have trained for years to help their patients. The creation of a Mental Health Care Plan is straightforward. There will be similar provisions in other western countries like New Zealand, Canada, and United Kingdom although the details may vary a little:

> A mental health care plan is a plan your doctor writes with you about treating a mental health condition. It helps you to access eligible allied health professionals like psychologists, social workers, or occupational therapists who can help you get better and live well.
>
> A mental health care plan can be useful for people with minor mental health conditions or very serious conditions, short-term concerns or long-term illnesses. You don't already have to be diagnosed with a mental health condition to talk to your doctor about making a mental

health care plan.

A mental health plan can help you in a number of ways.

Creating a mental health care plan gives you and your doctor the opportunity to formally outline how you've been feeling, what your needs are and what results you would like. It also gives your doctor an opportunity to refer you to an appropriate treatment or support service.

Having a mental health care plan makes appointments with eligible allied health professionals more affordable. If you have a mental health care plan, for instance in Australia, you are entitled to a Medicare rebate on up to 20 individual sessions or group appointments with a psychologist, social worker or occupational therapist in a calendar year. To start with, your doctor or psychiatrist will refer you for up to 6 sessions at a time. If you need more, they can refer you for further sessions.[98]

Psychologists and allied health professionals

Your family doctor is in a position to refer you to a reputable clinical psychologist for your particular problems or those of your children, such as a child psychologist. For more on consulting a psychologist be sure to read chapter twenty-one. Professionals such as clinical psychologists, social workers and counsellors can provide an array of services to you which may include individual personal counselling, parenting programs and counselling for children. These services can be very helpful. They can assist you in supporting your health and wellbeing, and with the processing of negative emotions that undermine your effective decision-making.

Counselling by trained psychologists and counsellors can be accessed online, via telephone, and video. For instance, MensLine Australia provides services for men in the areas of relationships, fatherhood, anger management, and family violence. MensLine reports that when 'faced with a problem, men are often focused on solutions rather than talking about their feelings'. MensLine accommodates this preference and offers a practical approach to counselling while also encouraging men to deal with important emotional issues. The benefits of telephone and online counselling are particularly attractive to men who often find it tough to ask for help and may find face-to-face discussions about difficult issues confronting. Male clients appreciate visual privacy, an immediate response, and the anonymity enabling greater honesty in the client.[99]

People tend to find a psychologist through recommendation by doctors or a personal recommendation, or based on location, transport and parking convenience. Doing an internet search based on location, expertise and general perception of the psychologist's practice can also assist you. It would be wise to check your ideas with your doctor if you are considering consulting a psychologist. Again, be sure to keep the contact details of your psychologist handy, and the contact details of a back-up psychologist for when your preferred psychologist is on leave.

Child psychologist

Child psychologists are trained in a similar fashion to other psychologists. They choose to specialise in treating children. In today's world, children present to psychologists with a range of issues, one of which might be adjustment issues to parental separation. Another might be parental abuse, or trauma derived from parental conflict. A child psychologist can help your children through these issues. More importantly, they can help your children feel like they have an ally to help them cope with major changes in their life and, if high conflict has been present in the children's life, help the children recover. Obtaining a referral from your family doctor to have your children treated by a child psychologist is not just responsible parenting it is an investment in your peace of mind. Immediately addressing issues as they arise with your children prevents matters from getting worse.

That said, not all children find parental separation problematic. Children can adjust quite well. Children can be resilient. As a responsible parent who is committed to the wellbeing of your children, taking your children to your doctor will be one of the many tasks which will demand your attention. Should your child have specific cultural issues, a disability, mental illness, and/or particular adjustment challenges, be sure to inform your child psychologist so that they can include these factors in their treatment plan.

Crisis services

Crisis services do superb work on the front line. There are places to go for help for a range of reasons related to your separation. Government aid is one of them. In Australia, for instance, there is Centrelink, as well as emergency accommodation provided by women's refuges, welfare and religious organisations. However, resources are often stretched due to underfunding by governments.

If you are in a high conflict crisis situation, be sure to consult your family doctor. Your doctor can examine you and note any injuries inflicted on you. Your doctor can also write a report that corroborates your injuries. Get photographs of your injuries as visual evidence for your lawyer and the police. You may feel conflicted at the time about doing this, but do it anyway.

If you are a person of financial means, you may elect to pursue private sources of safety. Financial resources afford a measure of discretion and choice of helping agents. Such agents include private clinics which can be recommended by your primary care doctor, trusted family members and friends. Make sure you record your experiences and injuries. While you are experiencing raw emotions, you may not be thinking clearly. Records may prove valuable down the track.

Accountant

Your accountant is an important ally during your property settlement. Whether your accountant deals with your business finances or personal finances, they typically have a sound working knowledge of your financial affairs. Often, you and your Ex will have had the same accountant. All going well, the accountant should act as a neutral resource for both you and your Ex.

It is important to involve your accountant as soon as you can in your property settlement process. For example, they can be a great help in advising you on your assets and liabilities and how your business has been performing.

Accountants are also important resources for providing you with taxation advice. If you have a complex portfolio of property and investments, your accountant can advise you on the consequences that flow from the division of assets upon your property settlement. Do make sure that you get specific advice from your accountant before finalising any formal agreement with your former partner. Your future financial security may very well be improved by doing so.

If you do not have an accountant, finding a reputable accountant depends on their special areas of practice. There are many general accountants in the services market. General practice accountants can be found through personal recommendation or via colleagues. Sometimes in family law situations, forensic accountants are required to conduct audits or investigate asset hiding, and non-disclosure of financial information. Your lawyer will be able to recommend a reputable forensic accountant since lawyers generally often work in co-operation with forensic accountants. Depending on your situation, your government website may provide you with a list. Accountants are skilled experts. They will therefore have a professional association to which they belong. Check your local area by conducting an internet search. Accountants, however, are not financial advisors.

Financial advisor

If you are a person in possession of considerable assets, you will likely have a financial advisor. If you have not already been working with a financial advisor, you may not be aware of the important difference they can make to your decision-making in property settlement and thus, your financial future. As a result of your settlement, your financial resource profile will likely look very different.

The role of a financial advisor in family law situations is essentially to translate your (realistic) vision for your future financial security into decisions made during your property settlement negotiations. For instance, prior to and during your property settlement, your financial advisor can be useful in providing you with expert analysis of a variety of approaches to your property settlement and assess proposals by the other party. They do this to provide you with an array of options to meet your short-term and long-term financial goals. What's more, financial advisors can help you plan your financial future in detail once the separation has been completed.

Finding a trustworthy financial advisor is often made easier by asking close friends for their recommendations. Depending on your situation, your government website may provide you with a list. For instance the Financial Security Authority in Australia has a useful website—afsa.gov.au Your search for a reputable financial advisor can start with The Financial Planning Association of Australia—fpa.asn.au The list below provides relevant contacts for professional associations in other countries.

Financial advisors are skilled experts, but not all of them have experience with the complex financial issues of separation. Australia's most respected financial advisor, Paul Clitheroe, recommends that you ensure that your financial advisor is credentialed, has expertise, and that you make sure you are comfortable with the financial advisor to ask questions. He further advises that

> when you start searching for an adviser, it's a good idea to compile a list of questions to ask—like how they can help you, who will be handling your advice, and how much you'll pay for the advice. A reputable financial adviser will appreciate that you may not be in a position to pay for any professional services until your property matters are settled, and many will agree to defer their fee until then.[100]

List of Financial Planning Associations

Australia	
The Financial Planning Association of Australia	fpa.asn.au
New Zealand	
Financial Advice New Zealand	financialadvice.nz
Canada	
Financial Planning Association of Canada	fpassociation.ca
United Kingdom	
European Financial Planning Association	efpa-eu.org

Valuation experts

You will recall that in chapter two, several points were made about valuation experts. It is worth revisiting them here.

Valuation experts are useful for assisting you with the aspects of your financial settlement. You will very likely know there are various types of valuation experts, including real estate valuers (for residential and commercial premises), business valuers (who are typically specialised accountants) and property valuers (who deal with home contents/general property).

You will recall that real estate valuers (not real estate agents) can be jointly retained, if your situation permits. These days, both parties in low conflict separations can agree to retain only one valuation expert, thereby saving expense and controversy. For a fee, the valuation expert can provide you with their written valuation report on your property. Homes, investment properties or commercial properties are the items they advise on.

Your choice of business valuation expert is important. Business valuation is a highly specialised, complex field. Both parties are advised to agree on the one expert for reduced expense and dispute prevention. This task requires full and frank disclosure by both parties of all relevant information regarding the business. Otherwise, a forensic accountant who is experienced in appraisal may need to be involved. You can source recommendations from your accountant (or their professional association) for skilled business valuation experts.

Before you spend money on engaging a valuer, remember that unless both parties agree to a joint valuation, the other party is not bound to accept or agree on the value.

Friends and family

In the right circumstances, your friends and family can be a valuable social support resource who can remind you that they care, provide practical help, accompany you or simply just drive you to your meetings so you are relieved of the burden of navigating traffic and finding parking close by. This can be helpful in reducing anxiety. Friends and family members are there for your wellbeing and support, but *not* for your legal and medical (including psychological) guidance.

If trusted friends and family are sensitive and skilled, they can help you. They can help you remain on track in purposefully completing the tasks required to progress your settlement, offer the opportunity for some 'you time', and reassure you that you are not alone because they steadfastly refuse to allow you to self-isolate—your enemy to coping and recovery.

School

If you are a parent, your children's school can be an important resource for you and give you peace of mind. School staff, once informed of your children's new circumstances, can act as a back-up and provide you with feedback about your children's wellbeing and academic progress while at school. If there are identifiable changes in your children's behaviour, then school staff can let you know so any problems can be dealt with immediately, including arranging confidential counselling for your children. Do not be alarmed. *Not all children have problems.* Psychologists agree that a home with parents separated is better than being subjected to constant conflict. It is absolutely essential that you understand that children fare well when there is healthy, clear and direct communication with them about the changes happening at home.

Be sure to make a list of the school contacts for your children. Make sure you include the details for your children's teacher/s, and a school counsellor, amongst others.

Conclusion

There are many highly skilled professionals out there who can make an important positive difference to your settlement and Parenting Plan, and who can help you negotiate your way through the maze of coping and communication. Overpage, I have provided a template for you to copy and complete if you wish. Place it somewhere that is easy to locate.

Reach out.

Practical Sources of Help

Crisis Services

Police: ______________________________

Domestic violence service: ______________________________

Doctor: ______________________________

Back up Doctor: ______________________________

Psychologist: ______________________________

Back up Psychologist: ______________________________

School

Principal ______________________________

Teacher: ______________________________

School counsellor: ______________________________

Finance

Accountant: ______________________________

Financial advisor: ______________________________

Insurance broker: ______________________________

Banker/broker: ______________________________

Crisis and support services in Australia

I would like to take this opportunity to thank all of the wonderful people who volunteer and work at legal aid, women's legal services, support services and crisis services. The coalface is a demanding place and I most sincerely appreciate your skilled compassion and dedication.

Here is a list of services in Australia you might find useful .

Crisis Services in Australia

Service	Phone	Web address
Lifeline Crisis Support (includes multicultural support)	13 11 14	lifeline.org.au
RESPECT	1800 737 732	respect.gov.au
Relationships Australia (includes multicultural support)	1300 364 277	relationships.org.au
Elder Abuse Helpline	1800 353 354	eapu.com.au/helpline
Family Relationships Online		familyrelationships.gov.au
Family Relationship Advice Line	1800 050 321	familyrelationships.gov.au
Beyond Blue (depression and anxiety support)	1300 224 636	beyondblue.org.au
Rape & Domestic Violence Services	1800 737 732	rape-dvservices.org.au
QLife (counselling and referral service for people who identify as LGBTIQ+)	1800 184 527 or chat online	qlife.org.au
PFLAG Parents and Friends of Lesbians and Gays	see each branch	pflagaustralia.org.au pflag.org for other countries
MensLine	1300 78 99 78	mensline.org.au

Service	Phone	Web address
Federal Circuit and Family Court of Australia	1300 352 000	fcfcoa.gov.au
Mates provides support in the construction, mining and energy industry	1300 642 111	mates.org.au
Men's Legal Service (not for profit) see website for various branches available	1800 463 675	menslegalservice.org.au
Headspace (National Youth Mental Health Foundation)	see each branch	headspace.org.au
National Debt Helpline (free advice and step-by-step guidance on how to tackle your debts)	1800 077 077	ndh.org.au
Open Minds – assistance with mental health	1300 673 664	openminds.org.au
Financial Counselling Australia	1800 007 007	financialcounsellingaustralia.org.au
Financial Counselling Services (provides individual state services)	see each branch	afccra.org.au
Family Drug Help	1300 660 068	familydrughelp.org.au
Gambling Help Online	1800 858 858	gamblinghelponline.org.au
Kids Helpline	1800 551 800	kidshelpline.com.au

21
Sound investment: Working with a psychologist

The purpose of this chapter is to demystify the process of consulting a psychologist. This chapter demonstrates that the process is, like other professional relationships, one which involves working co-operatively with a trained professional to benefit from their expertise. Just as you draw on the expertise of your family lawyer, your financial advisor, your doctor or your children's teacher, the working alliance you develop with a clinical psychologist can make a positive difference for you. It can improve your ability to cope with the numerous demands of change and reshaping your life.

This chapter offers you opportunities to understand:

- the big picture of consulting a psychologist from a client's perspective
- the steps you can take to get the most out of working with a psychologist
- aspects of the working relationship
- how to position yourself to understand the difficulties you may be experiencing and work towards a positive outcome

Making the most of working with your psychologist

There are people out there who find the idea of talking with a psychologist about as appealing as a poke in the eye. You might even consider consulting a therapist as a sign of weakness. Alternatively, some of you have no problem at all unloading your woes on a trained professional who can help you understand your sense of hurt, guilt, betrayal, abandonment, grief, anger, anxiety, loneliness, relief, and/or confusion. Many of you can derive great benefit from working through your separation issues with a trained psychologist.

However, there may be some of you who have little idea what's involved in working with a psychologist. How do you get to see a psychologist? Typically, it will be your doctor who will refer you to a clinical psychologist. However, you can suggest to your doctor a psychologist to whom you would like to be referred.

Referrals are important and it is worth discussing the preferred qualities of your psychologist with your doctor. Such a discussion requires a little self-awareness. Would you prefer to see a male or female psychologist? If the issues you are facing require special expertise, discuss this with your doctor. For instance, if your separation has intensified an addiction or need for anger management then seeking specific help is appropriate. Do you want to see a psychologist with a specific first language and cultural background? If you are a victim of domestic abuse, be sure to tell your doctor so they can refer you to a psychologist who is especially effective in this area of work. If you prefer to see a psychologist experienced with same-sex or gender-diverse relationship issues, make this clear. It may be that your psychologist has not personally experienced domestic abuse, or is not from the same culture as you, or has had a same-sex relationship. But, just like your doctor, any psychologist worth their salt should have an understanding of, and empathy with, these issues. If they do not, they are not the right psychologist for you.

What does a clinical psychologist do?

It is important to understand what a clinical psychologist actually does. What is the role of a clinical psychologist? What do you say to them? How much of the private stuff do you need to tell them? How do they fix you? *Do* they fix you?

Let's use the current Australian context to illustrate. The training for clinical psychologists in Australia is generally similar to that of clinical psychologists in the United Kingdom, the United States, Canada and New Zealand. In Australia, the Psychology Board of Australia requires a clinical psychologist to have completed a four-year university degree and then a two-year period of practice under supervision by an experienced qualified psychologist. Some pursue further education to specialise in their field of interest (such as counselling, or clinical, forensic, health, addiction, weight loss, child abuse, relationships, sports, educational, developmental, organisational or community psychology). This further education typically requires the completion of a two-year Master's degree at a university. Fundamentally, the focus of the training of psychologists is on the scientific study of human behaviour, based on reliable evidence of effective interventions.

Psychologists' training also includes helping clients cope constructively with the ending of their relationships. In sum, when you consult a clinical psychologist about issues you are struggling with arising from your separation, you will be talking to a trained professional who knows how to help you. The most popular of these treatment approaches by clinical psychologists is cognitive behavioural therapy (often referred to as CBT). Generally speaking, cognitive behavioural therapy helps you change damaging thoughts, beliefs, attitudes and behaviours to positive ones which form the core of your wellbeing. Taking purposeful action to address these issues by working with a psychologist can be a great idea which merits your consideration.

Your first consultation

So, what does the actual situation of consulting a clinical psychologist involve? Very likely, your first step is to think clearly about what specifically you want to achieve from seeing a psychologist. Consider writing a list of the issues you are finding difficult and the outcomes you want to achieve. Going through the exercise of identifying the issues of concern and writing them down will help your thinking and start to shape your purpose in consulting a psychologist. It will help you to take this list to your first consultation with your psychologist.

But do psychologists fix you? Try to avoid thinking about psychologists as you would about a mechanic or plumber. It is essential that you understand this reality: *psychologists provide guidance on how to get you where you want to go.*

Your first consultation with your psychologist will typically involve a discussion of confidentiality, fees charged, and some essential personal information about yourself. At this first appointment, your psychologist will want to understand *why* you are seeking their assistance. This means that you will be invited to identify the issues that are troubling you. Typically, your psychologist will begin by asking, *'Hello _____. How can I help you today?'* This is your cue to identify the issues concerning you.

To fully appreciate the context of these issues, your psychologist may ask you about previous counselling experiences you might have had, your family background, social and personal relationships, and, depending on your responses, explore further specific issues with you. As part of this process, if you decide to continue seeking treatment from the psychologist, you and the psychologist will decide on a plan for future sessions. It is important that you understand that consultations with the psychologist are for allotted times, so you will not be able to discuss absolutely everything in the one consultation. Consultations typically last between forty-five and fifty minutes, although this varies across practitioners.

What will it look like?

The reality is there are no magical solutions in life. You are all different so the outcomes of sessions with your psychologist can vary. Your psychologist will *not* make any promises to you. No guarantees apply. What they *will* do is provide you with assistance to achieve the best result possible for you, in order to improve the quality of your life. To a large extent, whether you improve your life is up to *you*. You will find taking responsibility for your role as a client, and taking an active role in your therapy, *rewarding*.

Psychologists listen to you. They help you to understand the issues you are struggling with.

Not only will your psychologist listen to what is important to you, they will listen to your silences as well—what you do *not* talk about—with regard to the issue that brought you to their door. *Your psychologist will actively listen to you, question, give feedback, and share information.* They will take note of the surrounding information about your life and draw connections between that information and the issues that you are dealing with. They will encourage you to think about these links. They will encourage you to talk about what is important to you and your feelings about the issues you are dealing with. They will ask you probing questions. Through these questions you will learn more about yourself and how you react to the issues at hand. Your understanding will grow. So, too, will your self-knowledge and skills in dealing with challenges in your life. Therefore, trust your psychologist to help you and trust the process. When you get to understand an issue, its causes and expressions, you can go a long way to resolving that challenge or at least managing it so that you can live your life productively.

To enable your psychologist to help you, you need to be prepared to talk to them *openly and honestly.* Your psychologist is *not* there to judge you, however intimidated or embarrassed you might be at first. After a couple of consultations with your psychologist, when the strangeness has settled, you will likely find yourself relaxing into the process. This will happen surprisingly easily if you feel a 'connection' with your psychologist. Many psychologists have said that if you develop a rapport with your psychologist, if your psychologist appears to be genuinely interested in you, this is more important than the therapeutic approach used.

If, for any reason, you do not 'connect' with your psychologist and the situation is not working for you, be sure to consult your doctor for a more suitable referral. Discuss the issues with your doctor so that you can get to work with a psychologist in whom you have faith. At the risk of stating the obvious, be sure not to confuse discomfort due to exploring topics you find painful with dissatisfaction pertaining to the professional qualities of your psychologist. It is important to be aware from the get-go that the psychologist to whom you have been referred may not be right for you. Just as some lawyers can be unsuitable for particular clients, so can your psychologist.

There can be a number of factors which contribute to your dissatisfaction with your psychologist. Dissatisfaction can arise from:

- a growing sense that your psychologist is not genuinely interested in you
- obvious lack of life skills possessed by the psychologist
- the psychologist's lack of professional experience
- the psychologist's lack of knowledge of domestic abuse issues
- the psychologist appearing judgemental
- your sense that your psychologist does not fully appreciate the complexities of the issues with which you are dealing
- the appearance that your psychologist is unprofessional and defective in core skills such as listening
- the psychologist's lack of skill in cultural issues, language issues, and multicultural community dynamics
- the psychologist's incompetence and lack of training in disability issues, including disability discrimination and abuse
- the psychologist's lack of awareness or bias regarding LGBTIQ+ issues, including issues pertaining to same-sex and gender-diverse relationships and factors which contribute to relationship breakup.

This list of possible factors is not exhaustive. Learning what does *not* work for you can be useful in helping you to learn what *does* work for you. When discussing with your doctor the issue of a more appropriate referral to a psychologist, try to be as specific as you can about the factors which contributed to your dissatisfaction. What were the things that did not work for you? Such a discussion provides your doctor with valuable feedback about the psychologist and better positions your doctor to quickly engage their professional network to source a more suitable psychologist for you.

In action

Consider the following points to assist you in thinking clearly about working with a clinical psychologist.

Professional relationship

Know the nature of the relationship. It is a *professional* one in which everything you say is confidential (except threats to harm others). It is a relationship in which the psychologist has professional and legal obligations to satisfy while keeping you safe in the therapeutic environment. Be absolutely clear that you keep this relationship professional no matter how comfortable you might be with your psychologist. No matter how much you might like your psychologist, they are *not* your friend. Sometimes, it can be all too easy to be confused about this boundary, especially given that you are talking about intimate matters that you probably haven't shared with others. You and your psychologist are a team working to improve the quality of *your* life. Do not mess this up with blurred thinking about what your psychologist *is to you or might be to you* if the circumstances were 'right'.

A safe therapeutic space means that not only are boundaries between you and your therapist maintained, but that you can talk openly and honestly without fear of judgement.

Questions

There are questions which might be useful to ask at your first consultation. If you are nervous about consulting a psychologist, then why not consider writing questions down and taking them to your appointment? Note that while you will have questions, it is important that you understand from the outset that this is *your* process. Why have you sought help from a psychologist? What do you want to achieve with this help? Write these thoughts down and make a list of the questions you want to ask your psychologist.

Questions you might pose to your psychologist include some of the following:

- What therapeutic approach do they use and why?
- What goals are achievable?
- What will your therapy 'look like', i.e. what does it involve, how long does it take?
- Will there be work to do between appointments?
- How regularly should you consult them?

Do you come from a different culture than your psychologist? If this is a concern for you, ask your psychologist if they have negative assumptions about races, cultures and languages other than their own. Do they understand the cultural difficulties that might be in play during relationship breakups? And if you identify as LGBTIQ+, does your psychologist understand the issues which might be relevant to your relationship breakup? In short, ask your psychologist *how they can help you*. Make sure that you establish realistic expectations of what can be achieved with your psychologist.

Preparation

Preparing for your consultations is important. Setting some dedicated time aside to think through the issues you want to raise in each session has value. What do you want to achieve from your *next* consultation? What issues do you want to focus on? Decide what you want to talk about, write it down, and work through the list. It is quite acceptable to have questions rather than answers. It is also useful to write out some thoughts to take with you to your consultation. These notes will help you talk about the issues or ask the questions you might have listed on your paper.

Homework

Initiative is great. Talk to your psychologist about what 'work' you can be doing between appointments. Your psychologist will appreciate your commitment to dealing responsibly with your challenges and will likely have suggestions for you to consider. *Taking the initiative helps you feel in control of your life, even when you are struggling.*

Part of your commitment to making progress is doing your 'homework' between appointments, whether they be practical exercises, writing in a journal, reading chapters in a book, or practising certain techniques. Ensure that you spend time reflecting on what was discussed in your last appointment. Was anything missed in the discussion? Was anything raised that left you feeling uncomfortable? Ask yourself how you have been feeling since your last consultation. How have you been feeling generally? How have you been feeling in regard to the issues which ignited your need for psychological help? Has anything of note occurred since your last consultation? Are there still issues you are reluctant to discuss with your psychologist?

All of these questions merit your consideration in order to work through issues between sessions and be fully prepared for the next appointment. After all, you are paying for these consultations and preparation is not only part of homework, it is important to making the most of your time with a professional trained to help you. Ultimately, preparation and processing will place your progress front and centre.

Commitment

Your commitment to resolving your issues means that you attend all of your appointments. Try not to skip a session. Contact your psychologist's office to cancel (preferably with at least forty-eight hours' notice) should something prevent you from attending. Be sure to *reschedule* your appointment.

Process

Remember that this is a process which requires your commitment through attending appointments, doing 'homework', reflecting on what has been discussed and what needs to be talked through. To do this takes time, so be patient. Some of you will be less patient than others and want to see results immediately.

Working with a psychologist is a *process.*

Recognise that working through this process will deepen your appreciation of your own sense of self. Your sense of self will also grow by *being realistic* about what you can achieve in this process, so be sure not to sabotage yourself by setting yourself up for disappointment about what can be achieved and how many issues you can work on at once. Let your psychologist know if you are feeling frustrated at the pace of outcomes. Are there obstacles to your progress? Regularly reviewing your expectations and what your psychologist thinks can be accomplished can be helpful. Make sure your psychologist is aware of your expectations so there are no misunderstandings and that you are not working at cross purposes.

Discretion

It may be tempting to talk about your therapy sessions with others, or even throw a comment to your Ex in the heat of the moment which goes something like, 'My psychologist says that you …'. Try hard to avoid doing this. Your therapy sessions are important to your quality of life, so treat your sessions with the respect they deserve. Processing the content of your sessions requires deliberate and considered contemplation on your part. Your sessions with your psychologist are probably one of the few spaces in your life where you can be completely honest with yourself.

Of course, there are many more aspects to the working relationship with a psychologist, but if you are committed to doing the work required to improve your health and wellbeing during the difficult time of separation, a psychologist can make an important difference to how you cope, and even contribute to the soundness of the decisions you make during your legal process. To be able to talk through worrisome issues in confidence with a skilled, trained professional is an opportunity which can be positively life-changing.

Conclusion

Asking for help is a smart move. Drawing on the skills, abilities, knowledge and resources of others during a time of intense change is integral to acting with purpose. And it resoundingly demonstrates smart thinking. Engaging a psychologist is an empowering act. Move towards your finishing line.

SECTION 7
CONCLUSION

22
What to do with all the money you have saved on legal fees

I have written this book to enable you to change your life for the better.

You can now separate the smart way. You can take steps to save money on legal fees, such as thorough preparation (if you can). You can choose the right lawyer for you. You can shape the decision on the best legal pathway to separation. You can clearly instruct your lawyer with your goals in mind. You can budget for your legal and household expenses. And you now know how to communicate for outcomes.

The completion of your separation offers you a second chance in life. Do not squander this opportunity. Having been guided by this book, you are now in an excellent position to take charge of your life on your own terms. And this is exactly what you should do. Separation is an opportunity to start afresh. It offers you a chance to do better because you now know better. So, what should you do with all the money you save on legal fees?

Grow your resources

Financial security is the one thing that can take almost all the stress out of your life. *Be in control of your finances.* And key to being in control of your finances is making a plan that is realistic and achievable. *But you need to be committed to this plan.* Financial gurus like Paul Clitheroe and Scott Pape will tell you that any such plan must include saving, a constant awareness of your spending, reducing your debt, investing, and dare I say it – continued effort. And if you have a job, hard work.

Read Scott Pape's book, *The Barefoot Investor.*[101] This book is easy to understand and written by a financial advisor who knows his stuff. The book will help you take smart steps with your savings, however modest they may be. Pape's refreshing argument is that you do not have to be wealthy to be smart about your money. Moreover, you do not have to be wealthy to grow the amount of money you have, whether it be for your retirement or your post-separation life. You *can* achieve financial security!

Put down notes on paper to build a financial plan that reflects the future you can afford. If consulting a financial advisor is within your means, consult a reputable, trustworthy advisor who can work with you on developing short-term (one year), mid-term and long-term financial plans which reflect your priorities and the realities of your financial situation. You can create a map for yourself or a visual set of building blocks which represent the goals you have identified for your short-term future, your mid-term goals (the next five years) and your long-term goals (ten years and beyond). Your confidence will grow as well as your money during this process. Your goals will obviously depend on the amount of assets you have at the outcome of your settlement, the current financial demands on you, and your commitment to making a better future for yourself. And please, if you are a person of modest means, do not think that a positive financial future is out of your reach. This is not the case!

Financial self-protection

Financial self-protection is key to your financial security. Let's revisit this issue.

The importance of financial self-protection cannot be stressed enough during this process. Your planning for the future should include income protection insurance. You must maintain your ability to meet the unexpected. Income protection measures can vary between providers, so do your homework. Insurance companies consider age, sex and occupation when designing your income protection package. If paid work is a must in your life, then taking out income protection insurance can provide you with regular payments around 75% of your usual income (in Australia) should you become injured or sick.[102] Taking out this protection is also tax deductible in Australia.

You may need to check regulations in your state/country. Another form of self-protection is private health cover, the purpose of which is to help you pay your medical expenses. If you cannot afford the highest cover package, consider downgrading your private health insurance.

Consider Total and Permanent Disability insurance to cover illness or accident causing a permanent inability to work. Consider trauma insurance to cover one-off serious health events such as heart attack, stroke and cancer, to help cover costs and tide you over until you return to work. Your particular circumstances will direct the need for insurance.

Recall the measures suggested for those of you who might identify as 'silver separators'. Please refer to chapter three.

A last word

Well done! You have reached the end of the book. Thank you for taking the time to read it. I hope the information has improved your knowledge of how to conduct your separation process to save money on your legal fees with good organisation and a willingness to be an active participant.

If you found this book helpful, please spread the word. Buy the book for a friend. Buy copies and donate them to community organisations. We all know someone who is going through a separation. Use this book to lend people a helping hand.

Starting a new future need not be a terrifying venture. It need not be overwhelming. And it most assuredly need not make you live without the money that should be in *your* bank account rather than in the bank account of someone else, like your lawyer. Whether or not you have children, no matter what your background, your new life is yours to celebrate in your very own individual way. Such a future may include things that you could not or would not have done in the company of your former partner. New friends are out there, ready to take delight in your company. Adventures await, whether it be travel, a new place to live, new hobbies, and new pleasures to enjoy and give you a healing peace of mind. Separation is the opportunity for new beginnings. Why not see where they take you?

This book offers you opportunities to succeed in many areas of your life. Do not let your past define you. Let your newfound freedom take you to peaceful fulfilment. *You* can make this happen.

You can do this!

Acknowledgements

This book has evolved over a number of years. The people close to me have travelled this journey with me. They have fostered my determination to make life easier for those going through separation and divorce. In doing so, they have supported my commitment to advancing positive professional interactions between clients and family lawyers.

Showing clients how to save money during the legal process of their separation has been an important goal for me. Fairness, kindness and compassion have always been strong values in my life. I have applied them with insight throughout the communities I have interacted with, paid work I have conducted, my research and writing, and my entrepreneurship.

A number of authors and organisations have generously granted me permission to draw on their work for this book. Paul Clitheroe, financial advice guru and author of *Money, Marriage and Divorce*, you are an inspiring professional and so encouraging to others who want to contribute to the greater good. Your encouragement and leadership has long been important to me. Jess Hill, author of the superb book, *See What You Made Me Do*, did not hesitate to recognise the importance of this book. Jess, I hope this book helps people just as yours has. Clarissa Rayward, Principal of The Family Law Centre in Brisbane, kindly extended permission to draw on her book, *Splitsville*. Thanks also go to the extraordinary *Australian Institute of Family Studies*.Thank you to all the staff and researchers there who continue to provide quality reports and interpret the varied issues which impact on people and families in Australia. My thanks also goes to *Relationships Australia*. You have all permitted this book to help others.

To my editor Rebecca Wylie and book designer Luke Harris you have both been an excellent publishing team. You have both taught me so much.

Director of *WorldWide South Brisbane*, Matt Wibberley, and his production staff Nicholas Simon Smith and Michelle Nelson kindly gave me an insightful and fun-filled publishing learning curve.

There have been many friends and colleagues who have, over the years, extended kindness and support even though they were knee deep in their own work and other obligations. I thank them for their love and support.

Margaret Khoo read a draft of this manuscript with special care and with her characteristic professional excellence. You shared your brilliant mind, Margaret, and galvanised my thinking about the book and its value to people. Tony Hemmings introduced me to the explanatory power of the 'the man from Mars'. In doing this for me, Tony, you lifted the quality of my writing and the value of the exercises throughout this book.

Gail Allison, Principal of *Pathway Legal,* provided valuable feedback on an earlier version of this book. Gail has contributed to its quality through her sharp thinking and legal expertise. Her dedication to her clients remains inspiring. Gail, I have thoroughly enjoyed our many conversations about the realities of family law. Your mentoring and professional insights have played an important role in my own bid for professional excellence. Your belief in me and your unwavering belief that this book needed to be published has been so important.

Jennifer Franklin, Principal of *Franklin Family Law,* also generously read an earlier version of this book. You believed in this book and knew that it would help family law clients and family lawyers alike. You remained steadfast in ensuring this book would see the light of day and provided wisdom and encouragement when times were tough. Thank you, Jennifer for taking time out of your busy schedule to do this for me.

Others, including doctors, psychologists and past clients of family lawyers who humbly defied my wish to publicly recognise them, have also informed the value of this book.

It will not be surprising that a lawyer who writes a book to help clients save money on legal fees has been through her own separation. Thanks to those who were there for me at the time and kept me afloat. Your support made all the difference.

Those people close to me while I was writing this book deserve my heartfelt gratitude. Thank you most sincerely to my partner, who enriches my life each and every day. Words cannot adequately express the love and respect I have for such a unique and wonderful individual. My partner's patience, supportive feedback, critique of my ideas, intelligence, sharp wit and humour have made our home a laughter-filled, creative sanctuary. My partner's belief in me is a gift that I continue to respect and will never take for granted.

My mother Joy, or 'Joyful', as she was known, would have been proud of this book. I trust that it is a reflection of her integrity, compassion for others, and the sheer determination to raise her eight children to serve society well, despite the formidable challenges life threw her way. Joyful, my love for you and all I learned from you is in every page of this book.

My final recognition goes to my two little girls, Molly-Joy and Gidget. Long passed away, my girls gave my life new meaning. You both remain in my most sacred of thoughts each and every day.

About the author

Dr Adrian Callum is a lawyer, author and social entrepreneur who is based in Brisbane, Australia. For more than 30 years, Adrian Callum has engaged in social justice work, scholarship and practice.

She is the creator of the *Ex-Factor Conference* series which build clients' separation and divorce skills across Australia, the United Kingdom, New Zealand, Canada and the United States.

Adrian holds a Doctorate, a Bachelor's Degree in Law, a Graduate Diploma in Legal Practice, a Bachelor's Degree with First Class Honours in Humanities, a Certificate in Mediation, and a Certificate IV in Workplace Training and Development. She is a member of the Queensland Law Society.

Interested in discovering more about her work? All you need to do is visit her website **www.lawandlife.com.au**

Index

Endnotes

1 Hill, J. *See What You Made Me Do: Power, Control and Domestic Abuse*, Carlton, Victoria: Black Inc., 2019.

2 Hill: 5.

3 Hill: 9.

4 Hill: 9.

5 Australian Bureau of Statistics, *Marriages and Divorces, Australia, 2019*. Released 27 November, 2020. Retrieved 23 March 2021.

6 Australian Bureau of Statistics, *Marriages and Divorces, Australia, 2019*. Released 27 November, 2020. Legislation to allow same-sex marriage, *The Marriage Amendment (Definition and Religious Freedoms) Act 2017*, passed the Australian Parliament on 7 December 2017 and received royal assent from the Governor-General the following day. Same-sex marriage in Australia has been legal since 9 December 2017.

7 Clitheroe, P. *Money, Marriage and Divorce. Making the Most of Your Assets in Good Times and Bad*, Victoria: Penguin Random House, 2015, p. 72.

8 An early academic publication is Anne O'Brien's 'Left in the lurch. Deserted wives in NSW at the turn of the century' in J. Mackinolty and H. Radi (eds.) *In Pursuit of Justice*, Sydney: Hale & Iremonger, 1979, pp. 96–105.

9 Rogers, M., Pattenden, R., Pullen, J., Bickerdike, A. *Women and Separation. Managing New Horizons*. Victoria: Relationship Australia, 2017, p. 3. www.relationships.org.au/relationship-advice/publications/pdfs/women-and-separation-pdf. Retrieved 20 October 2020.

10 Bickerdike, A. Gee, T., IIgauskas, R., Melvin, T., Hearn, J. *Men and Separation. Navigating the Future*, Victoria:Relationships Australia, 2009, p. 1. www.relationships.org.au/relationship-advice/publications/pdfs/copy_of_men_and_separation.pdf Retrieved 20 October 2020.

11 Harland?

12 Unsatisfactory professional conduct includes conduct of an Australian legal practitioner happening in connection with the practice of law that falls short of the standard of competence and diligence that a member of the public is entitled to expect of a reasonably competent Australian legal practitioner. Professional misconduct is defined more broadly than unsatisfactory professional conduct and may include personal conduct by an Australian legal practitioner which does not occur in connection with the practice of law, but only if that conduct is so serious that it demonstrates the person is not fit and proper to continue as a member of the legal profession. See *Legal Profession Act 2007* section 418. Source: Legal Service Commission, lsc.qld.gov.au

13 Clitheroe: 105.

14 The American Psychological Association. See www.apa.org Retrieved 26 March 2020. I have applied these general resilience strategies to the issue of relationship separation.

15 This discussion is based on Harland, A. et al. *Family Law Principles*, 2nd Edition, Pyrmont, Sydney: Thomson Reuters, *2015* and Clitheroe, *Money, Marriage and Divorce*.

16 Clitheroe: 108.
17 Clitheroe: 108.
18 Clitheroe: 109.
19 Australian Institute of Family Studies, 'Divorce Rates in Australia', aifs.gov.au Retrieved 22 July 2021
20 Clitheroe: 55.
21 Clitheroe: 79–80.
22 Pape, S. *The Barefoot Investor for Families*, Sydney, HarperCollins*Publishers*,2018, p.246.
23 Clitheroe: 11.
24 Clitheroe: 11.
25 Pape, P. *The Barefoot Investor*, Milton, Queensland: Wiley, 2019.
26 Clitheroe: 33–34.
27 Australian Bureau of Statistics, 4125.0 - Gender Indicators, Australia, Table 10.1: Total number of hours and minutes per day spent on work (employment related and unpaid) (September 2017). Retrieved 29 September 2021.
28 Harrison,W. *From Hope to Strategy. The Anatomy of Negotiation.* Doncaster East: Pathfinders Downunder Pty Ltd, 2014, p. 51.
29 See for instance, Kahneman, D. *Thinking fast and slow.* New York: Farrar, Strauss and Giroux, 211
30 Ellis, A. *Anger. How to Live With and Without it,* Great Britain: Citadel Press Books, 1971, p.1.
31 This discussion is based on Alexandra Harland et al. *Family Law Principles.*
32 My thanks to Gail Alison, Principal of *Pathway Legal,* for an enlightening discussion regarding this issue.
33 Guest, R. 'Financial literacy is a public policy problem' 2017 theconversation.com. Retrieved 20 February 2020.
34 Clitheroe: 19.
35 Clitheroe: 20.
36 Ekman, P. *Telling Lies. Clues to Deceit in the Marketplace, Politics, and Marriage,* London: W.W. Norton & Co, 2009, pp. 41–42.
37 Ekman: 41–42.
38 Ekman: 41–42.
39 Ekman: 41–42.
40 Korda, P. *The Five Golden Rules of Negotiation,* New York. Business Expert Press, 2012, p.147
41 Korda: 147.
42 Korda: 148
43 Maurice Scweitzer, Wharton University, oid.wharton.upenn.edu/profile/schweitz
44 Stone, D., Patton, B., Heen, S. *Difficult Conversations. How to Discuss What Matters Most,* New York: Penguin, 2010, p. 200.
45 Stone, et al: 273.
46 Stone, et al: 273.
47 Ury, W. and Fisher, R., *Getting to Yes. Negotiation Agreement Without Giving In,* New York: Penguin Group, 3rd Edition, 2011.
48 Ury, W. and Fisher, R.
49 Ury, W. and Fisher, R.
50 Ury, W. and Fisher, R.

51 Korda: 153.
52 The following discussion is based on various sections within Korda, *The Five Golden Rules of Negotiation.*
53 Murphy, K., *You're Not Listening. What You're Missing and Why it Matters,* London: Harvill Secker, 2020, p. 4.
54 Korda: 153
55 Korda: 153
56 Korda: 153
57 Korda: 153
58 Stark, E. *Coercive Control. How Men Entrap Women in Personal Life,* London: Oxford University Press, 2007.
59 This table is adapted from Rayward: 187.
60 Harland, et al: 88.
61 Rayward: 195. This table is adapted from Rayward: 187
62 Harland, et al: 88.
63 This is adapted from Rayward: 210.
64 This discussion is based on Harland et al: 95–97.
65 Cited in Harland, et al: 96.
66 Harland, et al: 95–96.
67 Dr Jennifer McIntosh quoted in Harland et al: 96.
68 Harland et al: 96.
69 Harland et al: 97-98.
70 Harland et al: 98.
71 see Rayward: 197-210 and Harland et al: 91–92.
72 Harland, et al: 89.
73 Harland, et al: 89.
74 Based on Rayward: 216–217 and Harland et al: 89
75 Australia Bureau of Statistics, *Labour Force Status of Families,* 16 October, 2020. Retrieved 10 October 2020.
76 Harland, et al: 132, 135.
77 Harland, et al: 260.
78 Australian Bureau of Statistics, *Census of Population and Housing, 2016,* abs.gov.au/ausstats/abs@.nsf/Lookup/2071.0main+features852016. Retrieved 10 October 2020.
79 Harland, et al: 134.
80 Harland, et al: 149.
81 RSPCA – kb.rspca.org.au
82 RSPCA – kb.rspca.org.au
83 statista.com
84 Rook, D. 'Who Gets Charlie? The Emergence of Pet Custody Disputes in Family Law: Adapting Theoretical Tools from Child Law', *International Journal of Law, Policy and the Family,* Volume 28, 2, 2014, pp. 177–193.
85 divorceresource.com.au/resources/in-the-news/new-pets-risk-programs-helping-keep-pets-safe-family-violence, Article dated Friday 14 April 2017 Retrieved 4 February 2021.
86 Annette Howard, Founder of Safe Steps Safe Families South Australia, 'Animal Justice party calls

for family violence law reform for victims and their pets' 1 March 2021, abc.net.au. Retrieved 22 August 2021.

87 'Animal Justice party calls for family violence law reform for victims and their pets' 1 March 2021, abc.net.au. Retrieved 22 August 2021.

88 Babcock, P., 'Are pets assets or part of the family? States are passing laws that give judges a longer leash in divorce custody proceedings', *American Bar Association*, 2019, 6, abajournal.org. Retrieved 4 February 2021.

89 Rundle, L. 'Charting a course through Client Costs agreements', *Proctor,* May 11, 2020, pp. 34–35.

90 Rundle: 34–35

91 Ball, M., Hayes, S., 'Same-sex intimate partner violence: Exploring the parameters' in B. Scherer (ed.) *Queering Paradigms,* New York: Peter Lang, 2009, pp. 161–177.

92 The Lifeline website can be found at lifeline.org.au

93 lifeline.org.au

94 Fileborn, B. *Sexual violence and gay, lesbian, bisexual, trans, intersex, and queer communities.* Australian Centre for the Study of Sexual Assault (ACSSA) Resource Sheet. Melbourne: Australian Institute of Family Studies, 2012. Retrieved from aifs.gov.au/acssa/pubs/sheets/rs3/ 30 January 2021.

95 For the first pathbreaking sociological study on stigma, see Goffman, E. *Stigma. Notes on the Management of Spoiled Identity,* New York: Simon and Schuster, 1963.

96 2011 NSW Report AIDS Council of NSW.

97 Calton, J., Cattaneo, L. B., Gebhard, K. T., 'Barriers to help seeking for lesbian, gay, bisexual, transgender, and queer survivors of intimate partner violence', *Trauma, Violence and Abuse,* 2015.

98 Queensland Health health.qld.gov.au/news-events/news/what-is-mental-health-care-plan-how-to-access-Queensland-Australia.

99 mensline.org.au/about-us

100 Clitheroe: 92–93.

101 Clitheroe: 92–93.

102 Clitheroe: 213.

www.ingramcontent.com/pod-product-compliance
Lightning Source LLC
LaVergne TN
LVHW052305200926
848481LV00002B/466